# Raising Your Own Children

# Raising Your Own Children

## A GUIDE FOR STAY-AT-HOME MOM WANNA-BE'S

### Carey Keavy

**To order additional copies of this book, contact:**
Xlibris Corporation
1-888-795-4274
www.Xlibris.com
Orders@Xlibris.com
23129

# Contents

FIRST AND FOREMOST, TO MY SAVIOR,
JESUS CHRIST, WHOSE UNSELFISH SACRIFICE ON
THE CROSS HAS EMPOWERED ME TO TRANSFORM MY
EXISTENCE, TO MY HUSBAND, JEFF, WHOSE LOVING
SUPPORT OF ME AS A WIFE, MOTHER, AND BEST FRIEND
HAS BEEN MY REFUGE, TO MY CHILDREN, JAELEN,
JADRIEN, JAMISON AND JACE, ALL OF WHOM I HAVE
BEEN BLESSED TO RECEIVE FROM HEAVEN, AND
ALL OF WHOM I COULD NEVER LIVE FULLY WITHOUT,
TO DAVE, WHO ENCOURAGED ME TO TAKE MY LIFE
SERIOUSLY... TO "PUT A FLAME UNDER MY BUTT",
AND TO MY MOTHER, NANCY, WHO NEVER
DISCOURAGED MY DREAMS.
I LOVE YOU ALL.

# Introduction

There are many reasons why this book began. The most important of those being the realization of the importance of my role as a mother in my own children's lives. As I worked closely with many young children in my children's entertainment business, I had observed the perplexing demeanor of children who had spent a majority of their time in daycares. Many had seemed to lack a sense of security and confidence. Some were overly aggressive, others extraordinarily clingy. I had begun to arrive at the point where I found myself being able to automatically pinpoint whether or not the children at each event had been in daycare or not. A curiosity was born, and a passion stirred.

This book is not intended to condemn, but rather to assist those who have a desire to dedicate their lives fully to the raising of their children by forcing their business lives to fit in around their children and not to fit their children in around their business lives.

I solidly believe that most mothers truly desire to be home with their children, but either just can't see how this is a possibility given their current situation, feel emotionally overwhelmed by being with their children all day, or find their identity primarily in employment.

There is pressure from every angle in our time for women to *have it all*. I will set out to prove that *having it all* is a myth. When one has a whole pie, and *has it all*, there is no pie left over for anyone else. The family unit and your children will always be the losers in the game of *having it all*, as well as your health, sanity, and peace.

I hold some very strong opinions and convictions regarding mothers and the roles they should play in the lives of their children. This book is merely my voice, and one woman's opinion. Take away from it what you need, and leave what you don't need.

This book is not an easy solution, and will require effort on your part. I will attempt to provide support, information, and formulae for you to use in your life to help you quit or reduce your job hours and increase your family time with money-saving tips, brain-changing philosophies, and downright straight talk.

Please join me in a journey of facing yourself, your wants vs. your needs, your priorities, your parenthood and your life. In the meantime, you may just realize all you have, and all you can really live without.

# Chapter One

## NOW WHY THE HECK WOULD

## I WANT TO DO THAT?

*"Dedicate some of your life to others.*
*Your dedication will not be a sacrifice.*
*It will be an exhilarating experience because it is*
*an intense effort applied toward a meaningful end."*
—*Dr. Thomas Dooley*

We all face challenges and struggles that are unique to our own personality types, but each of us has a common goal in mind here—to spend more time with our families, and to spend less time being overscheduled and stressed to the gills. I'm so thankful you are allowing me a small chunk of your mind in which I can implant "stay-at-home mommy propaganda!" Let's begin that process—together. Go "mommy power"—*MOMMIES—UNITE!*

# Tackling The But

*"Our doubts are traitors, and make us lose the good
we oft might win by fearing to attempt."*
—*William Shakespeare*

One small thing we must address before beginning our journey is a tiny, yet powerful three-letter word that you may find rearing its ugly head during this transition from work to home. The well-known ogre of a word is "but." The power of this word has kept many from accomplishing their goals and living the life they've dreamed of living.

How can such a miniscule word prevent you from your goals? Let's take a look at a typical conversation within a person's mind—where the word "but" is invited:

"I really want to stay home with the kids—*but* it's next to impossible. I mean, I think I could do it—*but* I'd have to stop getting my nails done. I think it's a great idea—*but* I know my husband wouldn't hear of it—I won't even ask him about it. I would like to quit my job—*but* I'll never have any time to myself. I think we could pay off our debt—*but* it's so overwhelming to think of it."

The word "but" seems so slyly innocent, doesn't it? Can you see its overpowering influence here? Observe how it carefully slips itself into the unsuspecting sentence to justify whatever it is you are doing. Notice how the "but" cancels out everything said before it: "I know I shouldn't have said that mean comment to my husband—*but* he was being such a jerk!", "I know I shouldn't eat this double-chocolate-dipped whipped-cream éclair, *but* I've already eaten fourteen, so what's the difference?" We say "but" in these sentences to justify doing what we know is wrong for us to do—and it makes us feel *so* much better—*instantly*! Isn't "but" a great word? No, no, no, my estrogen-laden friends! "But" must be viewed as the *enemy*! Repeat this after me: "MY BUT IS MY ENEMY!" (Just make certain there isn't anyone around when you say that—they may send you away in a straitjacket!)

Pay close attention to your thought processes as you ponder the decision to alter the course of your family life. Notice when the "enemy word" jumps out from nowhere and attempts to devour every last bit of hope you have left for your dreams! Yes—there will be arising circumstances that make this all seem impossible—there will be obstacles and times of frustration along the way. You *will* hear the enemy word. Your husband may say it. Your friends may say it. Your mother may say it. *You* may even say it—but just by being aware of the word and its power—you're already two steps ahead. Don't let a measly little three-letter word stand before you and time with your children. Only *you* can give the word its power—by surrendering yourself over to your doubts and giving up.

Just by reading this today, it shows that you have a desire to change your current situation and your life, making more of your time available to your children and family. Although that change will sometimes prove to be uncomfortable and stressful, I urge you to "keep your eyes on the prize" in the same way that a racing greyhound keeps his eyes fixed on the rabbit dancing in front of him to provoke the race. Your children will know that they are an absolute priority in your life . . . *this* is your prize! Is this prize worth the pain? You have to make the commitment to see this prize come to pass no matter how tough it will *temporarily* be. If we never make the effort to achieve our dreams, and instead allow the "buts" of life to stand in our way—how will we ever know what might have been on the other side? Taking a risk is often necessary in order to find what lies on the opposite side of the fence. Are you ready to take a risk for your children? Are you prepared to peer over the fence to view your new life on the other side?

## *Self-Discovery:*

Be keen to that pesky three-letter word as it's bound to jump all up in yo' stuff! Doubt is the enemy and fear fueled *only* by your willingness to harbor it in your spirit!

# Put Your Breasts to the Test

*"Can a woman forget her suckling child,*
*that she has no compassion on the son of her womb?"*
—Isaiah 49:15(KJV)

For those of you who have nursed a baby in your lives—one thing is made very clear right away during the process: if you happen to skip a feeding or two while away from the baby . . . suddenly you find that your once drooping, flab-infested breasts have become the most enticing things your husband has laid his eyes on since Pamela Anderson left *Baywatch*. Dolly Parton ain't got nothin' on you, baby! (Please *Parton* the use of incorrect grammar, friends!) Yes, engorgement looks fantastic in a string bikini, but in reality, it's a pain-filled ride in a parking lot full of speed bumps. The intensity of engorgement pain is on a level close to that of childbirth itself!

Let's go back to that design stuff and that God guy. He has designed our bodies to perform amazing feats. It's an awesome thing to think that a woman's body can nourish her child on breast milk and nothing else for over a year, if need be. A baby will eat every two to four hours for the initial part of the first year and maybe every four to five hours in the second half. Even if you did not nurse, your body was still designed by God to carry out the same astounding duty.

When babies are designed to rely upon their mothers for nourishment every few hours, where does an eight-hour day *plus* commuting time fit in with this design? If God wanted us to be away from our babies for extended periods of time, why do those who nurse have breasts that swell up like pre-eruption melons of Mount St. Helens when away from their infants?

When our skin touches the intense heat of a flame, our body is equipped by God to feel pain as an indicator that something is wrong—and if we are wise, we will then turn away from the source of the pain. Our breasts feel pain because something is wrong—our babies are gone. God did not create breast pumps—humans did. He intended for us to be with our babies.

### *Self-Discovery:*

We have been blessed with an amazingly constructed body. It functions beautifully and wonderfully all on its own— we never have to tell our hearts to beat—they just thump and bump around all by themselves. God *designed* our hearts to do this. God also designed a life for a woman. Are you living outside of God's design for you? What kind of pain is rearing its ugly head in your life as an indicator that something is not quite right? Depression, anxiety, stress?

## Is Five Years Too Much?

*"Life becomes harder for us when we live for others,*
*but it also becomes richer and happier."*
—*Albert Schweitzer*

When we choose to fully dedicate ourselves to raising our children—leaving our careers behind in the interim— we need to remind ourselves that the state of childhood is a *temporary* situation. They will soon trek off to school at the ripe ol' age of five, leaving you the freedom to once again pursue your career during their school hours.

The first five years of a child's life, known by child experts as "the formative years," are essential to a child's emotional well being. It is a time when they are forming their opinions of the world around them. The sense of self-development during this time is critical, and it holds the key to children's life-choices throughout their years on earth. It is during this time that they decide who they can trust and who they simply cannot, and just exactly how they fit into this giant planet.

In his book, *Bringing Up Kids Without Tearing Them Down*, Dr. Kevin Leman notes separate studies performed by two psychologists who take a closer look at the innate mothering patterns of birds. In one study, Konrad Lorenz discovered that the process of teaching the young to follow the mother duck was completed within the first twenty-three hour period of their lives. If the ducklings had been absent from the mother during those crucial first hours, the babies would have been unable to learn to follow the mother duck. Lorenz coins this phenomenon "imprinting." Another study, carried out by psychologist Konishi, found that songbirds also learn their songs in very short periods of time. He found that once the song was learned, it was irreversible and could never be unlearned. These findings also showed that if the baby songbird missed out on the period in which the song was taught, the song would never be learned at all. (1)

It is also interesting to note the spectacle of "false imprinting," which occurs when the animal's mother either dies or has abandoned her young. The offspring is then raised by a surrogate mother—which can be an animal of the same species or of another kind entirely. I have personally seen photos of baby ducklings that were falsely imprinted by their stand-in mommy—a dog! It was the strangest thing to see a devoted line of meandering, yellow puffballs faithfully following a canine! Human children are also capable of being falsely imprinted by someone other than their mothers. This occurs when they are placed in daycare during the first year of life—one of the most crucial bonding and developing seasons for children.

It is plain to see how the plan of God intended baby

birds to be imprinted by their mothers. If the mothers were somehow unavailable during the time of training, the babies were the ones who paid the price. The offspring were forced to go through life without the knowledge that was their inherited birthright—*if* they were fortunate enough to survive at all.

As the duck and songbird were designed by God to be imprinted by their mother, how much more is a human baby designed to have the same right. It is every child's right to be lovingly raised by its mother. A decision made by a family to separate a baby from his or her mother is contradictory to God's design for the life of a child and a woman. *[See Titus 2:4-5]* It is in the best interest of *every* child to be alongside its mother for the first five years of his or her life.

The average lifespan of a woman is seventy-nine years, with some living to under the average age and others surpassing the average into their late nineties. Let's take the low average, and understand that five years of sacrificing employment totals 6.3 percent of the lifespan. If the person lives to be ninety, which many do, the total time of sacrificing employment would be a little less than that percentage— coming in at a whopping 5.5 percent. When you consider these facts, do these percentages still seem overwhelming? Is 6.3 percent of your life too much to ask of you?

The years we sacrifice to be home with our children can occasionally feel like a prison term in a smelly, whiney cell. When we choose our children over our careers and personal goals, it can be a time of emotional difficulty for us as mothers. We can constantly feel compelled by the world to accomplish *more*—to do something more "tangibly apparent" than *only* taking care of small children. These pressures can sometimes cause us to question the validity of the sacrifice. "Is it all *really* worthwhile? When I go back to work, will this gap in my résumé be frowned upon? Will others still see me as important after I leave my career behind? Will I see *myself* as important when my days consist of changing diapers and wiping noses?"

These questions and fears are certainly genuine, and it is true that we *will* lose some of the things we perceive as worthy in order to gain the new life we desire with our children. Some seemingly good things must always be sacrificed in order to gain the *greater* good. We cannot expect to be slim and trim while we hold the habit of food overindulgence. We cannot expect to have a large savings account if we maintain a practice of over-spending. We cannot expect to have a happy marriage if we continually speak disrespectfully to our spouses. We need to come to the realization that we will *indeed* experience the loss of some privileges and benefits as we choose to sacrifice our time and careers for our children. We as mothers need only to assess whether or not we think raising a portion of the next generation is more important than the benefits we will likely lose.

It is entirely impossible for we as women and mothers to *have it all.* This is a lie that has been passed on to us by the feminist movement. Some areas in our lives must be sacrificed in order to *have it all* and unfortunately, the first sphere that seems to be forfeited is the parenting arena.

Do you believe that your child is worth the measly five years of sacrifice? Is five years of surrendering your career really just a crazy notion not even worth discussion? Yes, it may cause you to step out of your comfort zone, and it may be somewhat difficult to accomplish your goal—but isn't your child worth it? What do you believe your child deserves?

## *Self-Discovery:*

If you think about it, selfishness is the one thing that causes a majority of the problems in our relationships. Becoming a parent can reveal selfishness like no other instance can! Admitting that we are selfish can be a difficult thing—but once we realize that we have put our own needs above what is best for our children and families—we are well on our way to change. Search yourself prayerfully—ask God to reveal your true motives for the choices you are making in your life. Although you may be able to list several benefits that your full-time job brings to the family, is your decision to remain in the work force honestly "all about you"?

## The Daycare Dilemma

*"If you bungle raising your children,*
*I don't think whatever else you do well matters very much."*
*—Jacqueline Kennedy Onassis*

I don't need to tell you that the financial cost of daycare is extremely high. If your child is in daycare now—you are already well aware of the considerable chunk this expense takes out of your budget. Daycare can come with a hefty price tag, but quite frankly—the providers certainly aren't paid enough for all that they do. Their true job is to replace mothers, and the art of mothering cannot possibly be measured at an hourly rate of pay.

The monetary cost of daycare can be tremendous, but it is certainly small when compared to the emotional and physical costs that daycares cause the children who are in them. Let's take a look at some of the evidence I've collected regarding the negative effects that daycare has been found to have on children:

- In one study, seventeen percent of the children who were placed in childcare for more than thirty hours per week (during their first four and a half years) exhibited behavioral problems and aggression as reported by the teachers in their kindergarten classes. (2)

18

- A small but significant link has been found between time spent in daycare and how positively a child interacts with his/her mother. (2)
- The number of caregivers and the amount of time children spend away from their parents harms parent-child relationships, thus weakening cognitive and emotional development. (3)
- Children in daycare have shown a fifty percent higher chance of repeated ear infections. (4)
- In a nine-country study, children in daycares were more likely to have a history of poor hearing, tympanostomy tubes, tonsillectomy, or adenoidectomy. (5)
- Children under two were more likely to be hospitalized for lower respiratory tract illnesses if they were in daycare centers with more than six children. (5)
- Young children in daycares are slightly less likely to bond well with their mothers than stay-at-home children. (6)
- A Finnish study of 2,568 children found that children in daycare centers accounted for 85 percent of the pneumonia cases in one-year-olds. (7)
- A child who has not experienced strong attachment to a primary caretaker during his first two years of life—with the first year being of primary importance—is not likely to be able to establish and maintain stable intimate relationships, such as close friendships or even marriage. The earlier the disruption of the attachment process occurs, the more serious and long-lasting the damage will be. (8)

Dr. Stanley Greenspan, a professor of psychiatry and pediatrics at George Washington University Medical School and author of *The Irreducible Needs of Children*, states, "A warm, loving human relationship is very important for intellectual development. Children form their capacity to think and self-image based on these back-and-forth interactions. Fewer of these are happening, because families are so busy and more care is being done outside the home. Studies [show] that for all ages, 85 percent of day care is not high quality." (8)

For working moms, the hours spent at home are harried and few, leaving many moms wishing they had more vitality and time to invest into their families. The family unit suffers the consequence of an absentee mother. Marriages do not receive the attention they require and deserve. The child is deprived of an early bond with his mother, natural maternal nurturing, and the emotional availability of the mother during her work hours. The human imprinting that should be carried out by the mother is then unnaturally performed by the caregiver—because the imprinting still takes place.

The bonding and imprinting process for the child becomes even more problematic when he is placed in a typical daycare center, where the average rate of employee turnover is over half of their staff each year due the combination of low wages and high stress. (9) The child first experiences the loss of the mother for attachment purposes, and then bonds with a caregiver, only to lose that caregiver, and the next, and the next, and so on. The result produces a child who has a difficult time forming meaningful connections to anyone due to excessive emotional loss, and who also has complications with trust and self-worth issues. Why trust anyone when they'll just leave you?

Of course, there are other choices in childcare situations, such as the nanny, a smaller in-home daycare, or a grandparental caregiver. I would say that these are a small step up from the infant and toddler-farm daycare centers, giving children a *bit* more stability in their lives. Let's not deceive ourselves though—these conditions are still only a mommy substitute, merely giving our children *second best.*

If a parent chooses not to stay home with their children, the instance of grandparental childcare is usually the next most beneficial circumstance for the child. Nonetheless, this arrangement is not *completely* positive. Not only does this situation deprive the grandparent of a proper grand-parenting relationship—causing the grandparent to act as the main disciplinarian—it also unfairly places the full responsibility of raising the child onto the grandparents' shoulders. Mother abandonment and separation issues continue to be the core problem in any of these situations, and this cannot be remedied. When a child is separated from its mother, there will always be abandonment issues incurred—this is unavoidable.

Although not the most popular option, it is also possible for a mother to work full time outside of the home without the need for daycare or other parental substitutes. We can do this by deliberately choosing to work a shift opposite that of our spouse, so that our children will not be forced to spend time away from home with strangers. If we truly *must* work—this alternative is the closest thing to a win-win situation for everyone involved. The child is given the opportunity to bond with her parents, the relationship between a father and his children is strengthened, the guilt of child abandonment is lessened for the mother, and there is no added expense to the family for daycare costs. Of course, there are also disadvantages to this lifestyle. Some of the disadvantages include: the inability to spend an abundance of weekday time with our husbands, the sacrifice of having to work in a job other than what our specialized education implies (which could mean less self-satisfaction and the possibility of earning less money). We cannot *have it all.*

The concept of the institution of daycare was created to assist mothers who had suffered the tragic loss of a husband or who suddenly found themselves divorced. Having to earn an income in order to feed and clothe their families, these women were left with no other alternative but to place their children in daycares. Today, women of our society seem to view childcare as the *first* choice, while staying at home is viewed as living *counter-culture*—or only for the *lucky*. It is distressing to see that something which was once viewed as an unfortunate last resort has become known as the only ordinary, logical thing to do.

Sending our infants off to daycare does seem to be the norm these days, but the basic needs of babies and children still and always will remain the same. Simply because a society accepts a certain behavior as normal does not mean that this behavior is God's will or design for us.

The changing priorities of a culture does not cause children to magically evolve into sub-human beings who miraculously no longer need mothers to rear them! Children not only *need* to be raised by their mothers, but they also *want* to be raised by their mothers. Ask any child you know! Ask your *own* children with whom they would rather spend their days. Hmmmmmmmmmmmm . . . this is a hard one! Whom do you think they will choose? If you were a child, would you prefer to spend each day with a devoted mother who raises her own child solely because of her overwhelming love for him or her—or with a caregiver who only spends time with the child because she is *paid* to do it?

## *Self-Discovery:*

Don't leave this sub-chapter plagued with guilt and shame; those things are straight from the pit of H-E-double hockey sticks! God offers conviction from the Holy Spirit as a motivator to get our lives in line with His will for us. There is nothing that can be done to erase the things we've already done; only the power through Christ can transform and change the lives of His followers. God is a big enough God to cover your mistakes of the past—don't worry about the dead issues of yesterday—but begin *afresh* today!

# The Two-Income Society Sham

*"One of the weaknesses of our age is our apparent inability*
*to distinguish our need from our greed."*
—Anonymous

I believe that there may not be another statement spoken aloud that disturbs me more than this one: "We live in a two-income society—you just need to have two incomes to survive these days." Did someone just run their fingers down a chalkboard?! The idea of a family requiring two incomes to survive is a false belief that I consider to be based entirely on American greed and materialism. Most of us *can* survive on the income our husbands provide for the family—it is simply that we don't *want* to. Ready to throw this book at me yet? Of course, there are exceptions, such as the instance of a mother being forced to work because her husband only earns $6.00 an hour—I am not referring to those who are living in poverty—I am talking to Little Miss Middle–Class Mommy. OUCH—is that you?

Living on one income requires of us a surrender which is often painful. We are clever, crafty beings who are terrifically equipped to conjure up every excuse and justification on the planet—just so that we can keep our *stuff!* We thoughtlessly proclaim that we live in a two-income society—not because it is an accurate statement—but because many Americans have come to believe that a family cannot possibly live without the things that our society has deemed *necessary*—two cars, expanded cable, a huge home, expensive brand-name clothing, caller I.D., cellular phones, Internet access, and all of the other possessions in which we so blissfully indulge.

The basic needs of life are food, water, shelter and necessary clothing. (Although many nudist colonies may disagree with the last need!) If you have these needs met—you *can* and *will* survive. Anything other than what is listed above is *luxury*. That's right—*luxury!* How quickly we forget that only a hundred years ago, people lived meaningful lives when none of these things we take pleasure in even existed. Guess what? They *actually* had time to *enjoy* their lives! (What???!!! Enjoying life without being obsessed with the gathering of gadgets galore?) (Mrs. Keavy has officially gone off the deep—end now, folks!) Plumbing and running water—*luxury!* Electricity—*luxury!* (Now, she's slipped into a deep psychosis!) Vehicles—*luxury!* Computers—*luxury!* Telephone—*luxury!* (Okay, that's it! Sedate that delusional author—and make it snappy!) Please don't get me wrong— if we can afford these amenities—there is nothing wrong with enjoying them. My problem lies in the fact that many Americans have come to believe that we cannot exist without these luxuries in place. Isn't something amiss when we whimpering, spoiled Americans can't even survive a camping excursion? We cannot become so dependent on these amenities that we allow them to alter our values. We cannot permit ourselves to think that these lavish comforts are worth the trade-off for our children.

The sacrifices we sometimes need to make in order to do what is right are not always comfortable. The best choices and disciplines prove to be the most *uncomfortable* in the beginning—but the most *profitable* in the end. Exercising, eating right, saving money for retirement, and investing our time in our families are all things that are very uncomfortable to do—but the benefits they reap are on what the active doer keeps his mind set. How easily we give up when things first begin to feel uncomfortable. If the competition-winning body builder had given up when discomfort initially hit— not one muscle would have ever been developed.

Needing two incomes to survive is a choice we make by the lifestyles we choose to live. Two incomes are *not* necessary to survival—only to a survival full of luxury that is viewed as necessary. I realize that by living on one income, it can prove to be uncomfortable at times, and that you may need to go without some of the luxuries of the American life. Is it worth some loss to gain a victory in the end? Can you lose a few battles of the flesh now to ultimately win the war?

## *Self-Discovery:*

Comfort is what we've become accustomed to, but it is not always what is in the best interest of our families. If we are more concerned with comfort than with what is right, we will never succeed in anything that requires sacrifice. Are you willing to selflessly sacrifice your own desires for the sake of your children?

# Guilt to the Hilt

> *"Many people weigh the guilt they will feel against the pleasure of the forbidden action they want to take."*
> —*Peter McWilliams*

Guilt and shame are emotions that I have found to be a universal dilemma to those who work outside of the home for extended periods of time. Mothering is certainly a challenging enough task on its own—even before adding the extra ingredient of motherly guilt into the mixture. Why are so many working women plagued with these feelings of guilt? The *American Psychiatric Glossary, 7th Edition* defines guilt as: "The emotion resulting from doing what one conceives of as wrong, thereby violating superego precepts; results in feelings of worthlessness and at times the need for punishment." (10) Based on this definition, I must conclude that working mothers are inundated with guilt because they feel that what they are doing is somehow by their *own* internal moral definition—*wrong*.

In his essay, *Stages of Guilt Development*, researcher M.L. Hoffman discusses the positive effects of healthy guilt:

> "Healthy guilt is an appropriate response to harming another and is resolved through

atonement, such as making amends, apologizing, or accepting punishment . . . . Healthy guilt inspires a person to behave in the best interest of him—or herself and others and makes amends when any wrong is done." (11)

God has equipped us with the emotion of guilt to generate the awareness that we are doing something outside of His will for us. In the same way, He has also outfitted us with a huge reaction of pain as our skin is being pierced or a response of involuntary crying when we witness a sad event. Guilt is intended to be a motivating factor in our lives. We should utilize the tool of guilt in making the proper changes to create lives that honor the One who gave us life.

The New Age movement that is sweeping the nation says that guilt is a bad thing, but the Bible says that God's laws are written on our hearts. [Psalm 37:31] Conscience is a gift from Him intended to help us to live our lives without being forced to suffer the consequences that attend faulty choices to which we lost sheep gravitate.

Do you remember the last time you told a lie? It may have just been yesterday when your ol' Auntie Ethel called and you told your husband to say you weren't home. You little *devil*, you! Even though Auntie Ethel is a windbag full of triple espresso, a little tiny twinge of guilt *may* have hit you, whether you remember it or not.

Do you ever notice how each time you avoid Auntie Ethel's calls, it gets a little easier to lie about it? The Bible also says that our consciences can be seared. [1 Timothy 4:2] This happens when we continue to do the things we know are not right, regardless of our guilt feelings. The tugging at our hearts becomes less and less as we continue the conduct, quenching the tiny voice of the Holy Spirit. [1 Thessalonians 5:19]

The emotion of guilt—when ignored and buried—can

soon manifest itself in the way of physical, emotional and spiritual symptoms. Guilt can also lead to detrimental parenting patterns which can include: overcompensating for the lack of time spent with the child by buying too many gifts; allowing the child to stay up too late at night in order to spend time with him or her; showing extreme lenience in a child's discipline and diet; over-indulging the child with toys, entertainment and activities; as well as many other parenting habits that are not in the best interest of our children. In the Bible study, *The Forgiveness of God*, RBC Ministries shares how Psalm 32:3-4 of the Bible illustrates the internal angst of King David as he experienced the physical, emotional and spiritual results of guilt after killing Uriah the Hittite:

> "When I kept silent, my bones grew old through my groaning all the day long [emotional]. For day and night Your hand was heavy upon me [spiritual]; my vitality was turned into the drought of summer [physical].

Here are some ways we may be affected by guilt:

1.  Physical. Unresolved guilt may affect us physically. It usually manifests itself in one of these ways:

>> listlessness
>> imagined sickness
>> real illness
>> headaches, stomach disorders, vague pains
>> exhaustion

If we try to run from our guilt, immersing ourselves in work or turning to sin in reckless abandon, we will pay a price. Eventually our bodies will force us to slow down.

2.  Emotional. Psychologists and counselors see these emotional effects of guilt:

> depression
> anger
> self-pity
> feelings of inadequacy
> denial of responsibility

3.  Spiritual. Unresolved guilt may have the following spiritual effects on us:

> a sense of alienation from God
> inability to pray
> reduced fellowship with believers
> no feeling of joy
> inability to read the Bible

4.  Relational. A lack of forgiveness will have an impact on our relationships with others in these ways:

> irritability
> blaming others
> withdrawal
> profuse apologies
> inability to relax
> self-justification
> refusal to accept compliments
> outbursts of temper"

Denial and justification are also potent tools used by the human psyche. Both of these tools protect us from the torture of guilt and allow us to remain unchanged. They eliminate the constant tug on our consciences, which urge us to make necessary changes in our lives. The dictionary definition of denial is: "An unconscious defense mechanism characterized by refusal to acknowledge painful realities, thoughts or feelings." (12) It is a powerful enough tool to allow a pregnant teen to deny that her stomach has grown large over time. Even though she feels the child rustling within her womb, she refuses to admit its existence. Denial prevails in the mind of the drug addict as he destroys the lives of his loved ones, causing the addict to believe that it is *everyone else* who has the problem.

In every book or article geared toward the working mom that I have read, I have found the subject of overwhelming guilt to be the *most* emphasized topic included in each text. Every piece of writing offers tons of advice to the working mom—helpful instructions on how they can overcome the nagging sense of responsibility that is causing them so much grief. The mere presence of the frequently printed advice leads me to believe that tremendous guilt is a rampant obstacle that working moms must face daily. It becomes clear that the working mom must also utilize the tools of denial and justification in order to survive the time away from her children. If she did not use these valuable tools of the psyche, she would be either forced by conscience to quit her job, or the constant angst would eventually drive her insane.

Is it possible that you may have already moved into a mindset of denial or justification? Have you allowed yourself to feel the guilt feelings associated with working full time outside of the home, or have you stuffed the feelings somewhere deep inside? How can you recognize it if you have?

Prayerfully ask yourself the following questions:

- How do I feel about missing some of the major milestones (first words, first steps, etc.) of my child's life?
- How do I feel about my child forming a stronger attachment with their caregiver than with me?

- Will I regret the time I've spent away from my child when he/she is grown?

If, when first leaving your child with a caregiver, you experienced true grief, isn't it possible that in order to cope with that grief you needed to somehow assure yourself of the validity of your choices? Was it a statement of *justification* that helped you to remove the nagging feelings? Did you hang on tightly to the advice given by a friend, loved one, or author who reassured you that you were doing the right thing?

Parental guilt is something experienced by *all* mothers, whether they are at home or working full time. The real test is what we do with this emotion; whether we will give it consent to destroy and disable us, or if we will allow it to steer us into change. Discovering our personal methods of coping with guilt initiate a major breakthrough in our quest to be home with our children. It is essential that we know ourselves well, identifying our motivations for the circumstances we permit to transpire in our lives.

### *Self-Discovery:*

Allow yourself to prayerfully ponder your life and to feel the guilt regarding circumstances that God wants you to change. On a piece of paper, journal what God has revealed to you, and prioritize them in numerical order; asking for strength to accomplish these changes.

## Out With the Leftovers!

> *"For what is a man profited, if he shall gain the*
> *whole world, and lose his own soul?"*
> —*Matthew 16:26 (KJV)*

I have heard many people say that they work outside of the home so that they can give their children a "better" life than they had or to supply their children with the "best" in life. This mindset seems to be predominant with many parents who grew up in homes lacking financial means.

We all enjoy giving our children nice things—there is a natural satisfaction in this task. But we must ask ourselves— when we as parents are devoting forty hours of our week or more to a company, does this really constitute the best we can offer our children? Aren't our children truly being deprived of the best of their mothers when our jobs are the main drain of our energy resources? Aren't our children merely getting our stale *leftovers*? Is that really the best for them? Would you ever consider serving *leftovers* to your dinner guests?

What is the "best" truly defined as? One definition taken from the Webster's New World Dictionary is: ". . . the most one can do, the utmost, {to do one's best}." When we stop to think of what the best is that we can do for our children— does it really sound wholesome for us to say, "To give her Reebok sneakers at age three!" or "To be able to afford a ballet class when she is two and a half?"

If you hold a *materialistic worldview,* perhaps providing material things does seem to be the best you can do—giving your child the things you never had as a youth. Isn't it somewhat foolish to assume that by having the ability to buy extravagant material possessions for our children we are enabling them to have a better life? Are we certain that our children view having *things* as more important than having *relationships* with their parents? Have we asked them what they think? Is it really reasonable for us to assume that the things we can provide for our children are more valuable than the building of solid relationships with them?

Sacrificing ourselves—our plans, our ambitions—and temporarily replacing these goals with the aspiration to devote ourselves to our families and children seems to me the *most* we can do, the *utmost,* to do our *best.* What does it mean to sacrifice ourselves? It simply means to view our jobs as mothers and wives as the most important ministry and privilege we will ever have. It suggests that we find a way to fit our business lives around our children, not fit our children around our business lives. It denotes the call for us to place the *needs* of our children and husbands *first* in our lives. "Oh my,"—you may say—"but what about *me*? What about *my* needs?" (It's *not* about you!) True fulfillment comes from knowing you have lived your life honoring all those for whom you are responsible for and by doing what God has called you to do. When we honor our families *first*, we can then be at peace as we indulge in "me" time.

Call me a big-headed blue-footed booby, but I am perplexed to understand the woman who thoughtfully plans a pregnancy, waits patiently to birth her child, and upon the arrival of the baby, she then exclaims that she could *never* possibly make it as a full-time parent—something she's just not *geared* to do—she then proceeds to ship her newborn off to daycare before the infant has even had a chance to smile at her. Please forgive my arrogance, but doesn't that seem just as silly as spending nine months of planning, designing and building a beautiful new dream home—then after the building process is complete—suddenly deciding to allow someone else to live in the house? Then to top it all off—you decide to pay *them* to live there for you!

A scenario like the one above sounds completely ridiculous, doesn't it? Why does it seem so ridiculous to do this with a house—but seem entirely normal to pay someone else to raise our children for us? Do we think this seems absurd because we value the house more than we esteem the responsibility of child rearing?

If we as mothers are having difficulty giving up our careers for our children, we need to question the motives we have when choosing to become parents. Do we want to provide things for our children that we did not have because we secretly desire to relive our childhoods through them— or because these things are what *they* really want? Did we choose to have children to add them to our list of accomplishments—the fulfilling job, the house, the BMW, the 1.5 kids—or did we have children with a specific mission of ministry in mind? Did we have our children solely because of what they could do for *our* self-image and worth—or because of what *we* can do for *their* self-image and worth?

We fear that if we choose to stay home with our children, we will lose the freedom to provide the things for them that we view as important. It is true that for some of us, it will be more difficult to involve our children in activities or to buy them new things. No matter what your income level, I can assure you that if you commit to a little extra planning and time, you will find that your family will find a way to make these things happen. It may require you to plan many months in advance for vacations, sporting activities, or purchases. What?! You mean I have to use *delayed* gratification? Choosing to stay home does not sentence our children to a life of lacking. With good financial stewardship principles in place our families can have *most* of the things they desire and learn valuable lessons of self-discipline in the process.

Living only to provide material possessions for our children will not equip them as adults to change the world around them—it will simply instill a self-centered, materialistic value system within their spirits. As mothers, we have the opportunity to set an example of true Christian servanthood for our children—to unselfishly lay down our lives and desires for the sake of those that we love. This is our "best." Anything else is yesterday's liver soufflé. Give them the best—give them you.

## *Self-Discovery:*

Let's take a peek inside ourselves to find the *real* reasons why these things we see as a "better" life seem so much better to us. Are we merely attempting to live vicariously through our children? Have we caused *our* unfulfilled goals to become *their* goals? Pray and ask God to help you determine whether these things are in fact relevant, or if we are unknowingly attempting to be seen in a certain light by others.

## Quality Time, Schmality Time

*"I've been trying for some time to develop a
lifestyle that doesn't require my presence."*
—*Gary Trudeau*

We've all heard the old adage, "It's *quality* time, not quantity time." I have only one question for the author of this notion: right after coming up with this philosophy—did you also happen to see Alan Greenspan floating around the sky wearing pink tights, with a purple pig in one hand and a sparkly green leprechaun in the other? Perhaps this person was trying to overcome the guilt associated with the children in his own life, or possibly just trying to find his niche in a market of working mothers. Whatever the reason for the birth of this idea, I firmly disagree with it and then some.

What is *quality time* anyway? Spending time at Disneyland? Bending down on one knee while you look your child directly in the eye for an hour straight? Playing Parcheesi for hours on end? What exactly is this *quality time?*

Just as we discussed in the last sub-chapter, when humans begin to feel guilty about the choices they are making, and want to continue to do those things from which the guilt stems, there are only a few options they can choose. They can cease the behavior, which will ease the guilt immediately. They can choose to numb themselves with substances (or shopping!) to forget about the guilt. They can occupy all of their time with work and activities so they don't have time to feel the guilt. They can justify their actions by telling themselves a lie—which is a watered-down form of denial. I believe that the concept of *quality time* is one of justification used to alleviate guilt, and it works well—*all* too well.

How about if we do a little calculation here of the actual *quantity* of time that many working mothers are really spending with their children? Let's just take a look at an imaginary suburb-of-a-metro-city-dwelling family, in which both the mother and the father work professional day jobs from 8:00 a.m. to 5:00 p.m. Let's imagine they have only one child—a girl—and that she has been in daycare from the time she was six weeks old. Monday through Friday, this family awakens the child at 6:00 a.m. so they can leave the house by 6:45 a.m. After returning home at 6:00 p.m., the child eats, bathes and is in bed by 8:30 p.m.

Much of the child's time spent at home involves being lost in the shuffle of a busy cycle. During the week, the child is alongside her parents during the hectic rush of the morning ritual for forty-five minutes. She is also present for the frantic two hours before bedtime as they all rush around cooking, eating dinner, and getting baths out of the way. The weekends for the child may be at a more relaxed pace, as we will assume that this particular mother is very careful to contract for household tasks, shop online for clothing, and order her groceries through an online delivery service— all so that she can fully devote weekends to her child and husband.

Following this schedule, the child spends about fifty hours per week (factoring in the commuting time of two hours per day, traffic time included) away from home. Forty-five of those hours are spent in daycare, with the other hours spent on the road. During a typical week, these working parents will have seen their child for 3.25 hours per weekday, and 14.5 hours per weekend day: a total of 45.25 hours per week. The time spent at home is less than the time spent in daycare and in the car. In this lifestyle, out of a possible 365 days per year, the mother of this family will have ended up devoting 98 days of *quality time* to her daughter.

In the first five years of this child's life, the parents will have actually spent 1.34 years with their daughter—which accounts for about twenty-seven percent of the entire five-year span. The parents will have spent about forty-four percent of the child's waking hours with her, assuming neither parent has other pursued interests outside of work. But if they spend all of that time reading, singing and dancing with them—it must qualify as *quality time*, right?

In order to be fair and *slightly* scientific (I've already put on my lab coat and goggles), we must also calculate the total time a stay-at-home mother would spend with her child. Let's assume that this mother has one child, and that like the previous child mentioned, this child also awakens at 6:00 a.m. and has a bedtime of 8:30 p.m. Just to make things simpler for me, (Although I am wearing a lab coat and goggles—I do not claim to be a mathematical genius!) I am also assuming that the stay-at-home mother does not work at all, not even part time. During the child's waking hours, the mother is available 7 days per week, bringing the total number of hours spent each week to 14.5 hours per day, which comes to a total of 101 hours per week. This mother will have devoted a total of 219 days to the child out of a 365-day year. In a five-year period, the child will have spent a total of 3.01 years with her mother. This time accounts for one hundred percent of the waking hours of the child's life—and can be summed up as about sixty percent of the total five years.

The vital task of bringing a human into this world and preparing him or her for a productive life in God's service cannot effectively be done with twenty-seven percent of our time. Successful child rearing cannot possibly be accomplished if we continue treating it as an *afterthought* in our lives—taking care of everything and everyone else before we have time to consider what *our children* need. Would you ever be hired for a job after you gleefully told the prospective employer that you would fully devote *twenty-seven* percent of your efforts to the company? Would you ever have married your husband if he faithfully promised to dedicate an entire *twenty-seven* percent of his life to you? These things sound absolutely ludicrous, don't they? We would *never* say these things! Yet, when we choose full-time work over time with our children, isn't this what we are silently telling our kids each and every day of their lives? Sadly—they have never been given any other options.

## *Self-Discovery:*

Take this time to truly calculate the amount of time you are spending with your children and the amount of time you are allotting to work and other activities and obligations. Write this down on a piece of paper. The items with the most time next to them will serve as a gauge of where your priorities lie at this time.

# Leaving a Legacy

> *"The true meaning of life is to plant trees,*
> *under whose shade you do not expect to sit."*
> —*Nelson Henderson*

When we leave this earth, we may be buried in a fine-looking pin-striped Armani suit, with a fluffy red carnation in the lapel—but we will *not* be able to transport that suit to heaven. We will leave all of our earthly treasures where they rightly belong—on the earth. (Then to the Salvation Army, because no one in their right minds would ever want to wear our outdated elderly duds anyway!) We have no other choice but to leave everything we own here on the earth when we exit the planet.

God instructs us as wise parents to leave a financial inheritance for our children. [Proverbs 13:22] Leaving behind an inheritance is a Biblical idea straight from the boss' mouth—*but* does this only include a *financial* inheritance? We can and ought to leave a healthy bank account alive and kickin' after we're gone, but what about the legacy we've instilled in our children? Would not imparted wisdom and a good family structure be a more *valuable* inheritance? Won't our children need wisdom and stability to properly manage a financial inheritance?

Warning: MORBID THOUGHT ALERT! *All* of us will surely be *dead* in one generation and *most* of us will be completely forgotten in only three generations. Even if you are the president and CEO of *Most Important Company in the World Incorporated* and still don't retire 'till you're practically in the casket (like Strom Thurman), you *will* be forgotten.

Imagine any company in existence one-hundred years ago. Now, can you tell me who the president of that company was? (Let's leave out that Quaker Oats guy on the oatmeal box, okay? He doesn't count.) Do you know the name of your great-great-great-grandmother or grandfather? Unless you happen to be a devout history enthusiast, or a genealogy freak-a-zoid, odds are that you were unable to answer.

Think about someone you know who is living life today as an alcoholic. Take a look at his father and mother. Was one of them an alcoholic too? Keep going back through the family tree as far as you can. The person you know is probably not a first-generation alcoholic. This is likely a tradition passed on from generation to generation. The first alcoholic in that family left a legacy that may have gone on for seven generations or more—and may continue on into the future if not successfully overcome by current generations. Hundreds of years of alcoholism—begun by someone who probably had no clue as to what kind of future he was setting up for his children and grandchildren. This is the awesome power of a *negative* legacy.

Imagine if we set out to build our own *positive* legacies for our children, grandchildren, great-grandchildren, and their children. What would happen if we made it a point to live godly lives, and to set our priorities in a biblical order by placing our God first, our spouses second, our children third, our occupations fourth, and our community fifth? What if we took the time to build strong marriages so that generations to come would be impacted by the example we had set? What if we devoted our lives to the raising of our children and looked at a job as just that—*a job*—to bring food, shelter, clothing, and a few wonderful amenities into our lives?

How much can one do to change the world from the grave? The power of a corpse is a little limited, wouldn't you agree? (Unless you're Jesus!) But the power of a legacy can affect the world for hundreds of years after we have departed. Should we spend our time saving our money for Fabergé eggs that collect dust on the shelves, or devoting our time to changing generations to come? You decide.

## *Self-Discovery:*

Spend some time in prayer and ask God to show you the legacy He wants you to leave for your children. Write those things down and post them clearly as a mission statement for your parenting. When a decision is at hand regarding the family unit, refer to this mission statement. Does the decision line up with the legacy you want to instill? If it doesn't—just say "NO!"

# Chapter Two

## IT'S ALL ABOUT THE CHING-CHING

*"The real measure of your wealth is*
*how much you'd be worth if you lost all your money."*
—*Anonymous*

Each of us steps into the voyage with different levels of income and also with various financial circumstances to take into consideration. Some of our husbands bring in the big bucks, while others earn a modest salary. Some of us are single mothers looking to find a way to expand our time and money to accommodate our chaotic lives. Whatever the situation, money is something that needs to be analyzed, scrutinized, strrrrrrretched and brought to the table for discussion. We need to arrive at the place where our money becomes our slave, to do what we want it to do. We can be free from our slavery to the almighty dollar and then become its master.

# A Material . . . a Material . . . a Material World

*"What some people mistake for the high cost of*
*living is really the cost of high living. "*
—*Doug Larson*

Yes, even Christians can gain wisdom from a Madonna song! "We are living in a material world, and I am a material girl." Hmmmmm, let's ask ourselves this question gals—are we *material girls?*

Being born and raised as full-fledged Americans, materialism is sometimes extremely hard to discern. We have been so brainwashed by our commercialist culture—the lines between our true wants and needs have been dangerously blurred. Even our government lives repulsively beyond it's means, boasting billions in debt to other countries and to itself. It is not a wonder why so many are filing bankruptcy, divorcing and even committing suicide due to their state of overwhelming debt.

So, is it *money* that is causing this dilemma? In 1 Timothy 6:10, the Bible states: "For the *love* of money is the root of all evil: which while some have coveted after, they have erred from the faith, and pierced themselves through many sorrows." Based on this scripture, we can see that it is not the green piece of paper that is the problem in our world. It is the *love* of the paper and its power that destroys us. When we become greedy, buying things out of lust and surrendering ourselves to debt, we "pierce ourselves through many sorrows." Doesn't it feel that way when we get our credit card bill after thoughtless spending sprees?

What does materialism mean anyway? The *Webster's New World Dictionary* defines materialism as: ". . . the tendency to be more concerned with material than with spiritual or intellectual goals or values." Is this definition a little convicting, or is it just me? I never knew that the Holy Spirit could convict me using the dictionary! Based on this definition, when we place material goals above spiritual and intellectual goals, we are being materialistic. How many times a day do we find ourselves thinking about our hair, our clothing, our nails, our furnishings, our decorating, our vehicles, our bills, our paychecks, our stomachs, and our homes? Are we spending more time pondering these fleshly things than pondering the things of God?

Some of us are reluctant to quit our jobs because we know that we will have to surrender certain things in our lives. When asked why we do not quit our jobs to stay home with the kids, we find ourselves saying things like, "Well, I know if I quit my job, I'd have to sell my car. We wouldn't be able to afford it anymore." and "We could never stay in our house once I quit; we'd probably have to live in an apartment." Isn't materialism the origin of statements like these? Don't these replies indicate the materialistic conditions of our hearts? "But what comes out of the mouth proceeds from the heart . . ." [Matthew 15:18]

Have you ever had the experience of visiting the newly built home of a friend or acquaintance, then coming home to your palace, and feeling like Cinderella with her pumpkin-coach in nasty, tattered clothing? Before you saw her new home, you were perfectly satisfied with your house. Now, all of a sudden—you're talking to your husband about how you'd love to build a new house; thinking of cities which you could build, how many bedrooms it will have; and you've already decided just how many brushed-nickel hooks you're gonna put in that *huge* walk-in closet! This feeling is called lusty covetousness— an emotion that can intensely consume us if we are not watchful. It waits silently in the darkened corners of our lives—patiently waiting to see if we are willing to ensnare ourselves in it's grasp—so that it may direct our lives along agonizing paths of materialistic self-destruction.

Because greed and lust have been pesky traits of humanity from the beginning of creation, the Bible refers often to these common temptations. "Lay not up for yourselves treasures upon the earth, where moth and dust corrupt, and where thieves break through and steal: But lay up for yourselves treasures in heaven where neither moth nor dust corrupt and where thieves do not break through nor steal. For where your treasure be, your heart will be also." [Matthew 6:19-20] God knows us so well—doesn't He? He knows how corrupt our hearts are and how easily we stray when our eyes become fixated on fancy-schmancy material things. Jesus certainly knew what He was doing when He told his followers they could not bring anything— not even a change of clothes to follow Him.

Over the course of history, the sins of lust and greed have proven to be a problematic snare for mankind. "For all that is in the world, the lust of the flesh, and the lust of the eyes, and the pride of life, is not of the Father, but is of the world." [1 John 2:16] God has never caused the head-spinning sensation of greed. Greed is a byproduct of our sinful nature. Materialism consumes our thoughts, causing the focus and attention that was intended for God to be transferred onto the object of our affection. In plain and simple terms—idolatry. In even simpler terms—*sin*.

## Self-Discovery:

Take this time to confess materialism as sin to God. Ask Him to forgive you and to change your heart concerning material possessions, helping you to notice when the ol' trusty lusty feelings surface again.

# Here's the Plan, Stan . . .

*"Write the vision, make it plain upon tablets, so he may*
*run who reads it. For still the vision awaits it's time;*
*it hastens to the end—it will not lie. If it seem slow,*
*wait for it; it will surely come, it will not delay."*
*—Habakkuk 2:2 (RSV)*

When arranging to build a home, we would never begin the construction process without first preparing a reliable blueprint. If we attempted to build a house with nothing other than emotions and some Elmer's glue, the house would surely collapse in time. In the same way, in order for our transition from work to home to endure the test of time— we must also create a well thought-out design for the new adjustments we'll be making.

In order to be triumphant, the work-to-home plan requires many factors to be firmly in place. The most important of these is the *unity* of the husband and wife in the decision to come home. If your husband is supporting you in your resolve to quit your job, ask him if he will join you in the creation of a plan. (Come on now, he joined you in the creation of the kids, didn't he?!)

If your husband is reluctant or opposed to the whole thing, your first and most vital step is to commit yourself to diligently praying for the softening of your husband's heart. It is a natural response for a husband to feel fear when the financial sphere of the family seems to be in jeopardy. The opposing hubby's resistance is almost always fueled by the fear of the unknown—don't resent him for it—he's only human.

We as wives are called to be ministers to our husbands. We must never resort to using the tactics of manipulation or bull-headed force to attempt to change the minds of our spouses. We must place the responsibility of changing the heart and mind of our husband's solely on the work and power of the Holy Spirit. It is an act of complete arrogance for us to assume that we can perform the work of God Himself. If we are faithful to humble ourselves before God—crying out to Him for the desire to be home with our children—He will be faithful to honor our request. When we rely on God to change our husband's hearts, we are allowing a miraculous circumstance to occur in which the Lord can be given glory. Isn't this our *one* and *true* purpose for life, anyway?

In her book, *Me? Obey Him?*, Elizabeth Rice Handford speaks of the wife's *biblically* persuasive powers over her husband:

> "The scriptural principle is stated in Proverbs 25-15: 'By long forbearing is a prince persuaded, and a soft tongue breaketh the bone.' The word *soft* means "tender" or "timid." God says a ruler can be persuaded to change his mind by gentle, unselfish, persistent persuasion. So a man can be persuaded to change his mind when a wife appeals in the right way." (13)

In addition to your prayers, keep yourself occupied by creating a plan on your own. Use godly wisdom to determine the right time to present the plan to your husband. Having a well-prepared plan may help your husband to consider your plan and to view it as feasible.

Your husband may initially reject the ideas you have presented, but patience is the key here. You may have to approach him with the plan more than once. You will need to wait on God to open the door to your husband's heart. You will discover that when you allow God to pave your way, it is not nearly as exhausting as using ourselves as human steamrollers—*forcing* things to happen the way *we* think they should.

## Step One—Looking in the Mirror!

The first step in this process is to personally *know* the family's financial state. Although an annoying task, we must understand the household budget—the inflows and outflows of money. So . . . goest thou noweth to fetcheth all of your financial informationeth (pay stubs, bills, mortgage statements, etc.), and let's get started with a W-2 and a smile!

Let's begin by getting a piece of paper, and drawing three vertical lines in three equal columns. (See how easy this is?) Now, label each column as follows: "Incoming," "Fixed Outgoing," and "Optional Outgoing."

In the "Incoming" column, you will list all sources of monthly income, and the amounts they provide. Don't forget things like child-support, dividend payments, or the rent payments the mice give you for allowing them occupation in your home. Now, add the figures in the "Incoming" column, placing the total at the bottom of the page. In the "Fixed Outgoing" column, list and label the monthly amounts of your *required* obligations. Fixed obligations are those that cannot be ceased because they are necessary to modern survival (like electricity), items required by law (car insurance), or payments that cannot be terminated unless the loan is paid off. More specifically, this column will include things like mortgages, insurance costs, car payments, utilities, boat payments, college tuition, fuel costs, credit card payments, grocery shopping, *needed* clothing expenses, loan installments and much, much more! (Sounds like an exciting infomercial, doesn't it?) As with the "Incoming" list, add these numbers and scribble the total on the bottom of the page.

In the third column, list your "Optional Outgoing" requirements. These are things like, oh, say, cable television, Internet access, bi-weekly trips to the nail salon, cellular phones, call-waiting and other phone fluff, gym memberships, book and tape clubs, hobbies, magazine subscriptions, private-school tuition, trips to the hair salon, restaurant/fast-food eating, costs for lunches at work, business-related clothing expenses, etc. These are things that are nice to have, but that can be easily eliminated from the budget, if need be. Expenses such as lunch costs, frequent restaurant eating, and hefty second-car fuel expenses will no longer be necessary once you've quit your job. Add the row and write the total at the bottom of the "Optional Outgoing" column.

Now, here's where those third-grade math skills come in. (You know—the one's you said you'd never use?) Subtract the "Fixed Outgoing" and "Optional Outgoing" figures from the "Incoming" total. This sum reveals to you exactly how much money you *currently* have left each month after paying all of your expenses. (Let's hope you have *some* left!)

Are we ready for the most *frightening* part of all? In the "Incoming" column, it's time to *remove* the money you receive from your job and work the totals up again. (Zoiks!) This new total is the *income* we will have to work with in our *new* budget. Now, take the new income total and subtract the other two outgoing columns from it. This figure is what you have will have left over if you continue the "Optional Outgoing" list once you quit your job. It may be a *negative* figure—but don't despair. Now, subtract *only* the "Fixed Outgoing" from the "Incoming". This number represents the amount of money you will have left once these optional things are removed from your budget. If it's still negative—that's all right now, cowgirl, 'cause we ain't yet finished, lil' buckaroo!

## Step Two—Trim Those Split Ends!

Luckily, it doesn't take a genius to figure out that when we *earn* less—we must *spend* less. Now comes the part that everyone enjoys most—removing all unnecessary items from the "Optional Outgoing" column, and possibly even some from the "Fixed Outgoing" list. We do this to cause the amounts we are *spending* to be less than what we are *receiving* into the home.

The removal of all unnecessary items from our list can be a somewhat painful process. Although it seems strange, there is a subtle grieving process that occurs when we choose to let go of things in our lives. My husband Jeff offered this nugget of wisdom in a recent situation we encountered, "If it's uncomfortable—it's probably the right thing to do. If it feels good—it's probably wrong." This idea makes no sense whatsoever to those with carnal minds—because the ways of God are completely opposite to the ways of the world. A quick reminder before we move on—the necessary items for survival are as follows; *oxygen, food, water, shelter,* and *basic clothing.* Do I need to repeat myself? Okay, I'm trusting that you'll keep this fresh in your mind as you review your list. (Be aware that the things that you *really* love to do and have will find themselves suddenly evolving into oxygen or food, so be cautious!)

We will begin the journey by removing all *obviously* frivolous items. I like to refer to these things as "fluff." Fluff can be defined as: An item or service which makes your life more *comfortable*—but if removed, will not cause any members of your family to *die.* Using the above definition, go to your list now and remove all fluff by crossing it out. (*Refer to the chapter "Secrets From a Scrimping Scrooge" to find out ways to replace some of this fluff with free and cheaper alternatives.*)

After all fluff has been successfully annihilated, work your figures up again. Is the outgoing less than the incoming yet? If it is, you can stop now. If it isn't—we are going to need to move on to the "Fixed Outgoing" list in step three. We may need to create a plan for removing some of these things from the list.

Please remember that anything we own with a loan obligation to a lender can be sold at any time. The loan can then be paid off with the money earned from the sale. We can then save up to purchase a replacement item that is within the means of our *new* budget. If you have to go without a second car for awhile—*so be it.* Many families make one vehicle work for them—and if *temporarily* necessary, yours can too. Inconvenient—but wise!

You may need to finance your main car—as long as the length and terms of the loan are *within* your budget. It is not required that we own the most extravagant van on the car lot—we simply need to use it to get us from point "a" to point "b."

Some of our husbands earn an income that will allow us to keep *all* of the material things that we possessed before the decision to stay home. Many of us will have to make substantial changes in our lives. Some will even have to rid themselves of a burdensome mortgage—even if it is the payment for their *dream home.* The house, you can find or build again, but the child will soon grow into an adult and the time lost can *never* be replaced.

## Step Three—Just Two Inches, Please!

Now that you have successfully decided which fluff items must be kicked to the curb, we are now ready for step three. The nature of this next step will differ for each person, depending on what step two revealed.

### *Balancing act successful?*

If, after finishing step two, you have found that your budget balanced beautifully, step three is tendering your two-week notice—*pronto!* After performing the above financial evaluation, you may have come to the realization that your family has been indulging itself unknowingly in a lot of fluff. You may have also noticed that by eliminating job-related expenses such as travel, food, and clothing—your budget goes from the Wicked Witch to Cinderella in a flash!

### *Still more flowing out than coming in?*

If your outgoing funds still outweigh the incoming funds after you've made all of your fluff cuts—don't get discouraged. We have more cuts to go—it is now time to take a look at some of your "Fixed Outgoing" items.

Take a look at your "Fixed Outgoing" list. We'll start with

the least painful items first. Any boat, jetski, snowmobile or ATV payments? I know your husband will despise me, but these will need to be the first to go. The easiest way to dispose of a fixed payment is to put the item up for sale and then use the proceeds from the sale to pay off the loan. You will either need to put those items in your front yard with a "For Sale" sign attached to them, or quickly place some classified ads in the local newspapers and/or specialized publications. Some areas offer magazines that sell only boats or used vehicles. Utilize message boards at work and grocery stores to announce the items you're selling. You may need to try one method for a while, and if your item doesn't fly—try another. Don't forget, word of mouth goes a long way too. Now, rework your numbers—removing all the items you decided to sell from this list—how does she look?

## *Numbers still not quite right?*

Okay—time to get brutal! It's time to take some kung-fu grip action to that budget of yours! (Hiiiiiii-yaaaaaaaaaaah! Boy, I feel better now!) We're going to have to engage in some drastic steps here. Let's prioritize the cuts, and make them accordingly:

- You may need to sell the cars you own with a loan payment, and use the money from the sale to pay off your current vehicle loans. You can then proceed to buy a reliable used vehicle for your family by either paying cash (if you can) or by financing an inexpensive vehicle with lower monthly payments than you had before.
- It may be that once you've quit your job, the house you currently live in is much too expensive for your new family budget. If this is the case, you may need to chat with a realtor to find a less expensive living alternative. Evaluate how much space you *really* need. Do your kids

truly need their own bedrooms, or can they share? Does your family really *need* three bathrooms?

- If credit-card debt is your main problem, consider either refinancing your home (if you can afford to keep the house on your new budget *and* if you are sure you have dealt with the ROOT problem of the debt) or by calling your local consumer credit counseling service *(Check out this site: www.moneymanagement.org or search your local yellow pages for more info.)* This non-profit service will negotiate with your creditors for you. The end result is either paying no or very little interest to the creditors, with one monthly payment to the service who will disperse the funds to your creditors until the debt is paid. Jeff and I were able to pay off $10,000 in credit card debt, and I have a friend who paid off $25,000 in credit-card debt—both of us did it in about three years using this service.
- If you are having a problem with the budget because of private-school tuition, you may be able to qualify for scholarships from the school once you quit your job, depending on your husband's income. Also— don't forget to explore the home schooling option! (Just a *little* plug there!)

## *Find that you still need some extra money?*

If you have investigated all of these avenues, and still come up short, your next option will be either working part time on a shift *opposite* of your spouse, finding a part time job in which you can work at home, or starting your own part-time business from home. Notice that the words part-time were repeated several times? This is our goal, remember? Look at your budget totals, and determine how much you will need to earn in your part-time endeavor in order to balance the numbers.

Needing to work part time now does not sentence you to employment outside of the home *forever.* This may simply be a temporary situation needed to financially prepare you for your life of full-time "mommy-hood." Use this time to create a plan in which you can remove the financial obstacles from the road home to your children.

## *Still need to work full time?*

In the rare case that you would need to continue working full time, you can still do this without sacrificing your children's time with their parents. It is possible to find a full-time job opposite your husband's schedule so that daddy can take care of the kids while you are at work. When searching for a job, there are many shift arrangements available (swing shift, graveyard shift, etc.). Although a job that allows you to be with your child may cause you to work odd hours, may not be in your field of choice, or may not pay quite as well as your current job, making the switch has a humongous payoff for which you will never be sorry. We should make choices in our lives today that we will enjoy recalling many years from now.

For the next six months or so, you can slowly begin to tackle your financial challenges. Create a plan and circle the date you plan to quit your job on the calendar with a chartreuse marker. (If you don't know what chartreuse is—just use red.) Begin to implement your plan immediately. You may not be able to quit or move on to part-time right *now,* but six months is a feasible goal for most.

## *Self-Discovery:*

After all of these steps have been taken, you may be a little stressed out. You now have my permission to spoil yourself. Relax, have a great time—just don't put that good time on a credit-card, *girlfriend!*

# An Industry Made of Cottage Cheese

*"Perpetual devotion to what a man calls his business is*
*only to be sustained by perpetual neglect of*
*many other things."*
—*Robert Louis Stevenson*

When we take a look at the sometimes beloved and often despised woman of Proverbs 31, we can see a tremendous example of how God intends us to behave as wives and mothers:

"Her husband depends on her, and she never lets him down. She is good to him everyday of her life, and with her own hands, she gladly makes clothes. She is like a sailing ship that brings food from across the sea. She gets up before daylight to prepare food for her family and for her servants. She knows how to buy land and how to plant a vineyard, and she always works hard. She knows when to buy or sell, and she stays busy until late at night. She spins her own cloth, and she helps the poor and the needy. Her family has warm clothing, and so she doesn't worry when it snows. She does her own sewing, and everything she wears is beautiful. Her husband is a well-known and respected leader in the city. She makes clothes to sell to the shop owners. She is strong and graceful, as well as cheerful about the future. Her words are sensible, and her advice is thoughtful. She takes good care of her family and is never lazy. Her children praise her and with great pride her husband says, 'There are many good women, but you are the best!' Charm can be deceiving and beauty fades away, but a woman who honors the Lord deserves to be praised."—Proverbs 31:11-30 (CEV)

Whether you can't stand this woman or love her enough to snuggle with her, this woman is truly amazing and then some. To think she did *all* this—and never even owned a dishwasher! We each have different areas of talents, and not one of us will ever be *exactly* like her—but we can use her as a godly example and certainly strive to honor God with our lives as she did.

The bottom line is this Proverbs 31 femme fatale did not spend her time lying like a sloth on the couch, watching soaps, and eating fudge pops. (Bummer.) She was praised for the care she gave her family. Bringing in additional income was something she did in her spare time. Notice that the woman did not *own* the shop, but she made garments *for* the shop. She could not have owned the shop in her spare time—she would not have had any spare time left in that case. She may have gone to buy a plot of land with a toddler on her hand and a baby at the breast.

If you already have an idea for a new business, or are planning on bringing your job home, be realistic about the time it will remove you from your family. Some think that when they work at home, they will be free to spend huge amounts of time with their children. In reality, many at-home jobs and home businesses can severely decrease the amount of time spent with your kids, and cause the children to become a hindrance to you while you are trying to complete the tasks of your job. This is *not* what we are trying to accomplish.

Service businesses tend to be the most flexible of all the cottage industries, and usually require the least amount of money for start-up costs such as house cleaning, consulting, etc. The service you provide is usually scheduled by an appointment and can be planned around your husband's work agenda. The appointment can also be easily scheduled to revolve around your children's activities and needs. The best types of service businesses are those that do not require a great deal of preparation before the appointment. The less time for preparation—the more time for your family.

Providing home daycare is an option very often looked at by mothers who want to be at home. I would discourage this option for most moms unless this is absolutely their particular area of gifting, or their last resort. It is my opinion that home daycare requires an enormous amount of time and energy that should otherwise be spent on our own families—not someone else's. It is very easy to be emotionally spent on a daily basis, therefore leaving nothing but a crabby, exhausted mom and wife. If this is the *only* way for you to be able to stay home, then try it—but use it as a temporary bridge into something that needs *less* of you.

There are so many choices when starting a part-time business. Here are some tips to help to get you started:

- Take clues from your own personality in starting a business. If you are a performer at heart, bookkeeping would definitely cramp your style.
- Study the yellow pages to take a gander at all of the business types out there—you may just come up with a fantastic idea. If you find something interesting, don't hesitate to call the company owners and ask them how they got started. Most people love to share their stories. You may even be able to talk them into meeting with you—so they can show you how their business operates.
- Don't let the fear of failure paralyze you. You are not looking to become the next Bill Gates here, just to supplement your husband's income so you can be home with your babies.

Ask yourself the following questions:

- What kinds of things do people say I do well?
- What skills do I possess that could be helpful or entertaining to others?
- What items can I create to sell?
- What can I teach others to do?

If you decide that starting a business is the right choice for you, and you've come up with a superb idea—it's time to start researching! Go to the library or log on to your library website to reserve and check out books on the business topic. While you're there, locate some books about small-business operation and taxes too. (Boring, but necessary!)

Make a list of all the materials you will need to buy in order to start your business, and any licenses or steps you need to take for legal reasons. You can acquire the items and licenses over a few weeks or months with your current paychecks, avoiding going into debt to begin the business.

Contemplate what type of advertising will work best to promote your new venture. You may be able to advertise in specialized publications that focus on your specific market. For instance, if your business is geared toward children—you may be able to advertise in a local children's publications, or send fliers to schools or daycares. Make sure you tell everyone you know, and I mean *everyone you know* about your business. Word of mouth is a powerful tool, and may just be enough to get your business up and running—like eating fiber in the morning.

By getting a business phone line, most companies will list your business name and number in the yellow pages as part of the package. Call your local telephone company and ask what they charge for a business line. It tends to be rather expensive, but actually ends up paying for itself with the business it brings in. Some telephone companies do not require the purchase of a business line if your home is equipped with extra phone lines, or if you list a cellular phone number instead.

Below is a list of business ideas that may help you get started in the thinking process, and get that hamster spinning in that mental wheel of yours:

| | | |
|---|---|---|
| Freelance Writer | Consultant | Wedding/Birthday Cake Chef |
| Life Coach | House Cleaner | Instrument Lesson Instructor |
| Clown | Pet Sitter | Caricature Artist |
| Bookkeeper | Medical Coder | Mailing List Creator/Editor |

| | | |
|---|---|---|
| Tutor | Personal Assistant | Professional Organizer |
| Nanny | Vocal Trainer | Editor/Résumé Creator |
| Graphic Designer | Word Processor | Internet Store Owner |
| Wedding Planner | Face Painter | Community Education Instructor |
| Storyteller | Seamstress | Beautician |
| Wedding Singer | Songwriter | Self-Published Author |
| eBay Sales | Personal Trainer | Professional Speaker |
| Cosmetic Sales | Interior Decorator | In-home Pet Groomer |
| Party Planner | Drapery Creator | Faux Finish/Mural Painter |
| Website Designer | Workshop Facilitator | Craft Maker for Bazaars |
| Budget Consultant | Photographer | Photograph Album Organizer |

These are just a few ideas that I came up with off of the top of my head, but don't let this list limit you. The possibilities are endless. Happy hunting and break a leg!

## *Self-Discovery:*

Starting or running a business is not for everyone. Pray diligently about this before taking off on your own. If God's blessing is not upon it, the effort is just not worth it!

# The Joneses Filed for Bankruptcy

> *"The best things carried to excess are wrong."*
> —*Charles Churchill*

Now that your income level will be dramatically changed, there are mental adjustments that must also accompany this change. *Earning* less means *spending* less—living within our means.

We should all know exactly what the phrase "living within our means" truly is, but unfortunately, in a society such as ours—we must re-educate ourselves regarding this term. The intention of this saying is to teach those who have a yearnin' to *spend and have* to *save and wait* instead.

Choosing to stay at home with our children does not mean that we punish ourselves by wearing our socks thread-bare so that we can then reuse them as hair scrunchies—though we will be required to take a major look at our wants versus our true needs. There is nothing wrong with buying something that we want, *if* we can afford to do so and *if* the consequences of that purchase will not affect others such as if you are not able to tithe or give to your church because of your spending habits; if you are unable to quit your job to be with your kids because you continue racking up the charge accounts.

It is extremely difficult to live in our culture and not be tempted to live beyond our means. Most of the people you and I know are indulging themselves in every buying whim when given the opportunity. The concept of *delayed* gratification is one that has not caught on as a widely accepted way of life in America. Credit has been used as the lazy man's way of acquiring material possessions. With only seventeen years of easy payments, you can own virtually anything you desire—why would we opt for saving our money to purchase items with cash when it's just as simple as driving to the store with plastic in hand?

An exaggerated sense of entitlement in America is a rampant problem facing many today. If we look back only two generations, we see that the material wealth our grandparents possessed took them a lifetime to acquire. Most married folk would not buy a home until they were in their thirties or forties, and some never did. The generations of today practically come out of the womb expecting to have everything their parents have without putting in the hard work. That's exactly where using credit comes in—to replace the discipline of hard work and financial self-control.

Below are a few tips to help you begin the process of living within your means:

- *Use discernment.* Always keep in mind the distinction between the terms "want" and "need". I have found that some people have an extremely difficult time discerning these two ideas. Remember that a need is defined as necessary food (nutritious), water, basic shelter, necessary clothing (functional, non-duplicate) and oxygen.

- *Stick to your list.* Always use a list when going into a store, and more importantly—discipline yourself to stay on the list. Sometimes, I like to fill up my cart with impulse buys along the way, and give them to the clerk at the checkout line. I explain with a smile that I don't really need the items, and that they were impulse buys. The exhilarating rush of the purchase is still there—and so is the extra money in my checking account!

- *Bring a wad of cash.* Use cash when shopping for groceries and essentials and bring a calculator to make sure you have enough to pay for what's in your cart. Using cash can help you to stay on the list—avoiding frivolous impulse buying.

- *Try not to buy new.* When considering an item for purchase, always stretch yourself to imagine if you could possibly buy the same item *used* for a considerable discount on eBay, at a garage sale, thrift or consignment store, or if you could borrow the item from someone you know. If you are planning on buying a new item at $100.00, but could wait a week or a month to save $50.00 or $75.00 by just shopping around or buying used—isn't it worth it? Why spend more than you have to? There have been many items I have wanted to purchase, but then borrowed them from a friend instead. Let me tell you that most of those items ended up only being used once anyway, with no desire to ever use them again, like the ice cream maker, and the books I never opened . . . and the . . .

- *Keep your buttocks out of the stores.* Limit store visits to once a week, once every two weeks or even once a month. The retail store is not designed to be a place to help you keep your money in your pocket. There are tons of gimmicks and mental persuasions planted along every aisle with the purpose of distracting you from your list. It wouldn't surprise me if Eve wasn't really tempted in the "Garden of Eden", but in the "Target of Eden." Retailers count on each consumer to buy at least six percent of their purchases on impulse! This means that they plan for you to come into the store with a list of ten items, and to leave their store toting sixteen items out to the car. Why do you think these retail stores spend millions of dollars researching consumer buying habits and performing customer census? Maybe it's because they've been planning to throw a huge birthday party for all of their customers and want to give them all exactly what they want! Let's face it, they want your Benjamins, and they know that we women love to buy pretty, fluffy, colorful things that they place right at eye level.

- *Use the money = time spent theory.* When looking at a potential purchase, discover how many hours it takes you or your husband to work to earn the amount of money needed for the item. Example: If your husband earns $20.00 per hour, and you are considering buying a $300.00 dress and shoes that you may only wear once—your husband will have had to put in fifteen hours of work to buy you that dress. That is almost two full days of labor! If the store told you that they would be happy to let you have the dress and shoes if you worked in their store for fifteen hours, would this still sound like a good deal? Decide if the purchase is a good trade-off using this method.
- *Keep a running list of WANTED items.* Keep an ongoing list posted in your home of the items you wish to buy and the date you decided you wanted to have it. This

may include an item you spotted at the store during one of your mature "I always stay on the list" shopping trips! Make a commitment with your spouse—agreeing that you will discuss even the smallest purchase plans with each other. The rule is that items must be on the list for thirty days before being purchased. If you really want the item that badly, you can use the next thirty days to save up for it by setting aside ¼ of the purchase price each week for the next month. The funny thing is most of the things you have on the list will probably no longer interest you by the end of the month. How does that classify it? Impulse buy! Naughty!

- *Don't use retail advertisements as entertainment.* Search newspaper retail advertisements and catalogs only when in need of a *specific* item. That kind of entertainment will merely entertain your thoughts long enough to plant a seed of greed. I started noticing that every time I received one of those awesome clothing catalogs in the mail, I was completely dissatisfied with my wardrobe for weeks afterward, with my new wardrobe shopping list all filled out. It dawned on me that the day before the catalog arrived in the mail, I was happy with my clothing collection. I now have a standard catalog-throwing-away-ritual that usually begins with me yearning to browse its pages—but ends with the repetitious chanting, "My life was just fine before you came to my house, and it will be just fine after you're in the garbage!" This mantra is then followed by the swift descent of the catalog into the depths of the trash bin. *Adios!*
- *Don't fall for the devil's sneaky trap of justification.* "Oh, it won't hurt—It's just one little shopping spree on credit . . . you'll be able to pay that off in no time—and it's on clearance—you have to get it!" Please be

aware that no one gets into $50,000 of debt by going out and charging an S.U.V. Big credit card balances happen *one* charge at a time. What harm could come from the innocent, single little drop of a leaky faucet? But if the faucet drips into a plugged sink, and drips . . . and drips . . . soon you find a flooded house. These small sprees add up, and soon enough—you'll be going back to work to pay all the monthly obligations you racked up!

### Self-Discovery:

Ask God to show you the things within you that are rebelling against Him and His plan for your finances. Meditate on this scripture and ask Him to change your heart. Psalms 139:23, "Search me, O God, and know my heart: try me, and know my thoughts: And see if there be any wicked way in me, and lead me in the way everlasting."

# Credit-Card Trap

*"Think what you do when you run into debt;*
*you give another power over your liberty."*
*—Benjamin Franklin*

We've all heard the warnings about credit cards, haven't we? We've all seen people virtually destroy their financial lives by running up so much debt that they are then forced to file bankruptcy. We all know at least one mother who is forced to work outside of the home due to a state of overwhelming debt that haunts the family. We all know these circumstances are bonafide. So, why do some of us still *abuse* our credit cards?

In the same way that money is not the root cause of evil, but that the *love* of money is the cause—credit cards are not the problem. It is our mishandling of the privilege that becomes the problem. The problem lies in the ease of living outside of our means with these plastic little fiends. There are proper ways to use credit that can actually be to our advantage. We need only learn what those ways are and discipline ourselves to stick with the new knowledge that we acquire.

So many of us in America are living beyond our means. It certainly seems like a great idea for us to own nice things— until the point in which we realize the nice things actually *own* us! We willingly submit ourselves to the slavery of debt when we *demand* to have what we really cannot afford. So many times, we are willing to sacrifice our future for our present wants. A good rule of thumb is this: if you could not afford to save up your money for a period of time to purchase the item in question with cash, you cannot afford the item. OUCHY WOW WOW!

I am not against the use of credit, only opposed to the abuse of credit that runs rampant in our society. Our family uses an American Express charge card, which we utilize mainly for business purposes, but for personal reasons as well. This is a *charge* card, not a credit-card—which simply means that whatever we charge that month must be paid off by the following billing cycle. Talk about accountability! This card has helped us to stay within our means when it comes to charging, as we know we cannot charge more than we can afford to pay off in a month. It has worked very well for us. Another credit card we find it beneficial to use is a Best Buy card. We generally use this card to buy appliances and electronics for our home. Due to their program of six months without interest on most large purchases—we use this card to buy appliances and electronics for our home. Though we usually have enough money in our emergency fund to cover the purchases, we take advantage of the *free* money they are offering and pay off the balance before being charged a cent in interest. Our emergency money stays safe and sound in its rightful place—in our pockets earning interest.

If you want to stay ahead of the game, never charge more than you can pay off that month, and always pay your balance in full. This eliminates nasty finance charges and allows you to stay in control of your financial life. If you cannot afford to pay a purchase off in a month, then this is *beyond* your means, and you'd better start saving for the purchase instead. If you have a problem with this discipline, get an American Express. If you still can't handle it—take your credit cards outside, run them over three times with your vehicle, bring them back to the house, slice them into fifteen pieces with a paring knife, then double-wrap them in aluminum foil, duct tape the shiny package and quickly dispose of it in the trash receptacle. *Aaaaah, freedom!*

## Categorize Yourself

In order to help ourselves control our debt issues, it helps to know our tendencies. Listed below are a few different types of credit-card users and their traits. Try to find yourself in a definition and learn to put your guard up—resisting your bad habits. Heed James 4:7: "Submit yourselves to God. Resist the devil and he will flee from you."

## —The Unplanner:

If you are this type, you will find yourself explaining your credit card debt like this, "We have so much debt right now! If only the car hadn't broken down, and then the refrigerator took a dive. Then there was that trip I had to take to Alaska for my Aunt Bessie's funeral. We might not be in such debt if we didn't have all of these things happening to us at once!" If you find yourself digging into the credit cards on a regular basis for things which come up as emergencies, please refer to the sub-chapter, *Expect the Unexpected* to learn how to plan for such events. With a little planning, we can eliminate the need for such unnecessary debt-hole digging. Even a funeral trip can be paid for in advance with an emergency fund. That's what it's for—emergencies! Ask God for self-discipline—helping you to learn how to save your money and to have the mentality of a *producer*, not a *consumer*.

## —*The Joneses Wanna-be:*

If this charging style fits your debt problem, you may find yourself saying something like this, "Well, I know I shouldn't have charged this big-screen television, but I just fell in love with the one my best friend's husband just bought for his family room. I really *do* love it and we needed it anyway. Ours was too small." If you find yourself in this description, pray and ask God to reveal to you the motivations in your life and the condition of your heart regarding greed and lust. This is a self-worth issue. Ask God to show you who you are in Christ without material things and accomplishments attached to your name. Read scriptures relating to how God sees you and loves you unconditionally.

## —*The Impulse Buyer:*

If you are this type of debtee, you may hear yourself saying this, "Oh, I know I really couldn't afford it, but I saw this really cute skirt, and it was on clearance, so I just had to get it! I mean, it was thirty percent off. How could I pass that up? I didn't have enough money in my checking account, so I charged it." Does this remind you of yourself? If it does, ask God to help you in the area of self-control. I would recommend *not* carrying credit cards on your person until you have proven yourself worthy of this responsibility. Believe me—contrary to popular belief—your type needs to leave home *without* it!

## —*The Controlled Charger:*

If you never charge more than you can pay off in one month, and do it with self-discipline and keen planning, you can keep on truckin'! Your financial state is its own reward!

## *Arm Yourself*

Now that we know what type of credit consumer we are, we can move on to the *defensive* techniques on the money field. What can we do to change the rut into which we've fallen? How can we alter our paths and hearts to reflect God's design in our financial lives?

Let's take a look at a few scriptures regarding debt and borrowing:

> "The Lord shall open unto thee his good treasure, the heaven to give the rain unto thy land in his season, and to bless all the work of thine hand: and thou shalt lend unto many nations, and thou shalt not borrow."—Deuteronomy 28:12

> "For the Lord thy God blesseth thee, as he promised thee: and thou shalt lend unto many nations, but thou shalt not borrow; and thou shalt reign over many nations, but they shall not reign over thee."—Deuteronomy 28:12

> "Give to him that asketh thee, and from him that would borrow of thee turn not thou away."—Matthew 5:42

Upon performing a search of the word "money" in the Bible, so many scriptures came up that it was almost unbelievable! God obviously wants us to be equipped with wise instruction for our finances here on earth.

Based on the few scriptures that I have included above, my consensus is that those who borrow are not those who are blessed. The Bible calls those who are blessed as the people who have enough to lend and never have to borrow.

Having enough money to lend to others is an important Biblical principle. The scriptures also point out that when we are blessed, we shall reign over nations and they shall *not* reign over us. When we owe excessive debt to lenders—we reign over nothing! The lenders reign over our finances, and we are in bondage to them.

My belief is that if we truly desire something and then pray about it, God will answer our prayers if it is in His will for us to have it. He has done this for our family so many times that we have lost count. But there were times when I've prayed for something to happen, and then, instead of waiting on God— I've gone out and made it happen for myself using credit or another means. I have come to realize that whenever I did this, I just cut myself out of a blessing that God had already prepared for me. If we wait on Him, He will bless us—and sometimes in truly unusual supernatural ways.

Using credit wisely can be to our benefit and not our detriment. If we can simply learn to apply Biblical principles to borrowing—we can have a victorious financial life with the freedom to stay home with our children included. Financial bondage is for the birds!

### *Self-Discovery:*

Let's not make a mockery of Christ's sacrifice for us by willingly submitting to bondage! He has set us free! Let's be obedient to His word: "Stand fast therefore in the liberty wherewith Christ hath made us free, and not to be entangled again with the yoke of bondage."—Galatians 5:1

# Expect the Unexpected

*"If you can count your money,*
*you don't have a billion dollars."*
*—J. Paul Getty*

If you ask a group of people to trace the source of their credit-card debt, many of them will say they created the debt with "unexpected" emergencies. The mindset of many of these people is: "What was I supposed to do? It just happened and I had to pay for it *somehow!* Why does this kind of stuff always happen to me? Just when I was getting ahead! I have such bad luck!" Let me tell you frankly—*luck* has nothing to do with it!

We live in an imperfect world where things break down, and unexpected things happen. Please embed this fact into your brain! Your car is going to break down at some point, and your dishwasher is going to poop out too! These things are inevitable. Let's stop calling them unexpected things, and be honest with ourselves—they are expected things. If we are expecting something to happen—wouldn't we be fools not to plan for them? In Proverbs the Bible says, "A wise man plans." This refers to planning for emergencies, expected repairs and replacements as well as planning for your life.

You may find that when you are home with the kids and your income has been drastically reduced, you are almost always on the verge of financial despondency. When you fall behind, you can no longer rely on an extra paycheck to rebound you from economic ruin. Having a safety net is *essential* to the success of our decision to raise our children above all other things.

You may be thinking, "We can't even afford to live now, let alone save money too!" Believe me, we were of that viewpoint at one time too. We just started saving by faith, and it was then that we realized all of the money we were squandering away without even recognizing it. On my husband's blue-collar salary, we began by saving $100.00 per month in a money-market fund. In addition to saving around $350.00 per month for retirement, we are also able to stock away about $250.00 per month in our savings accounts. Emergencies *do* occur—as expected—but the money is there for us when we need it. We simply put our hands back to the plow and rebuild the account to prepare for the next expected event.

To open a money market account, either contact your bank, or a brokerage firm like Smith/Barney or American Express. Once you set up an account, most firms will allow auto-drafts for as little as $25.00 per month automatically from your checking account to the money-market fund. You may want to start there and increase over time. If you can afford more—then go for the gusto!

Keep in mind that this money is not for vacations or that new computer you've been eyeballing—but strictly for expected events. You can add extra money into the account to save for all the fun stuff, just make sure you earmark the allocations on a handy piece of paper. You don't want to steal from yourself and your future.

Financial experts say that one should have three to six-months worth of income in an emergency fund as an ample safeguard. If you just keep pluggin' away you'll reach your goal. You may have setbacks when expected events happen, but you'll just need to turn yourself around and rebuild your savings. You *can* do it!

## *Self-Discovery:*

If saving is something new for you—get on your knees before the Lord. Ask Him for strength and direction to accomplish this task. Start small—simply make an effort, and God will honor you, meeting you where you are. "I can do all things through Christ which strengtheneth me."—Philippians 4:13 (KJV)

# Chapter Three

## SECRETS FROM A SCRIMPING SCROOGE

Becoming a full-fledged tightwad is more exciting than any *Indiana Jones* movie you've ever seen! Frugality is a constant adventure—you are continuously on the alert—ever-ready for the next knock-your-socks-off deal to show up! You will soon find that your children and husband will join in the fun—a cohesive penny-pinching family glue.

If you were just persuaded by my thirty-second commercial for the tight-fisted life—let's now explore some of the money-saving ideas that will get you started on your *stimulating* quest to spend less.

## Appetites of the Tight and Parsimonious

*"Food is an important part of a balanced diet."*
—*Fran Lebowitz*

Eating is a basic human need—but it is not necessary for us to dip into the 401K every time we hit the grocery store.

Our family of six tends to spend about $100.00 per week on groceries and household items, and we serve up some pretty impressive meals!

We'll begin our tightwad trek with the unveiling of the S.K.I.M.P. (Secret Keavy Inexpensive Meal Plan) Our family kind of accidentally invented this system. Maybe we *didn't* invent it? Either way . . . if we catch you revealing our classified Keavy secrets . . . we'll be forced to dispose of you. The method consists of these steps: organizing your recipes, finding coupons and sales, menu planning and shopping.

## Gettin' Yo' Stuff Togetha

To begin the S.K.I.M.P. we'll need to gather a few supplies and you may already have many of the things needed. If you are currently using a recipe box or binder for recipes—it can be easily used for the system. If you don't already have an organization system, you will need to buy or find some simple things to begin:

1. A large plastic recipe box
2. A package of large lined index cards for writing recipes
3. A package of large unlined index cards for pasting clipping recipes
4. Plastic label tabs for the recipe cards
5. A good supply of yummy recipes (If you don't already have very many recipes . . . search magazines, newspapers, cookbooks, and ask relatives too!)

Okay, we will now label the blank index cards by attaching the plastic label tabs to them. Label them as follows:

| | | |
|---|---|---|
| Chicken | Breads | Ala Carte |
| Beef | Desserts | Salads |
| Pork | Beverages | Veggies |
| Seafood | Potatoes | Meatless Meals |

If your recipe organization system previously consisted of a drawer full of crumpled clippings, you can now staple or glue your clipping-type recipes to the blank index cards. You may wish to transfer your existing recipes onto the lined cards if they are in a book or on a card too large to fit in the box. Organize your recipes in the categories provided, the most important part being the separation of the different meats the recipes use. For instance, if you have a chili recipe that calls for beef, place this recipe in the "beef" category. If you already own a recipe box or binder full of recipes, you only need follow the last step of separating the recipes into categories.

## Snippin' and a clippin'

I know the thought of coupon clipping makes many of us feel like disgruntled postal workers. It's a task that none of us look forward to—I realize this! Please keep in mind that it only takes a few minutes of your time each week, and by making this small time investment, you can actually end up saving thousands of dollars each year. Sound more appealing now?

"But I don't have time to clip coupons!" You can steal small snippets of time to take care of coupon clipping—clip while you are going potty—clip as you supervise your children playing at the park—clip as your husband drives your family to church service. No excuses!

You can find coupons for food and household items in a few different places: the Sunday newspaper, in-store ads, the Internet, and even on the backs of your food cans and boxes. There are two different types of coupons; the *store* coupon and *manufacturer's* coupon. A store coupon is one that is offered by a particular store, and can *only* be used at that location. Manufacturer's coupons are offered by the companies that own the products and can be used at any store that accepts coupons. You can use both coupons at the same time on products, and save a lap full of funds this way. If the grocery store features a $1.00 off coupon for X brand sour cream, and at the same time, X brand sour cream offers a manufacturer's coupon for $.75 off, with the sour cream normally priced at $2.50, using both coupons to buy it, you pay only $.75! Manufacturer's coupons can also be combined with regular store *sales* too—not just store coupons.

Although our family is too cheap to subscribe to it, we have found the Sunday newspaper to be the best source for coupons. It contains both the store *and* manufacturers' coupons. If you don't subscribe to the Sunday paper, ask someone you know who does subscribe if they will allow you to have the manufacturers' coupons and store ads each week. My husband actually swings by our favorite grocery store on his way home from work to pick up the in-store ads. (Bless his sweet heart!)

## I'll Have the Salmon ala King, Please . . .

The basis of this system is to plan your weekly menu around the meats that represent the best deals of the week at the grocery store, using the sales ads and coupons. We will create a weekly menu consisting of seven meals.

Your first step is to bring a pen and an index card to your freezer to take inventory of the meats that you currently have lurking there. List the meats on the index card. Your goal for the week is to have 5-6 meats available for dinners. If you already have that much in your freezer, you will not need to purchase meat at the grocery store this week. Simply begin creating a weekly menu, using the meats you already have on hand. Also, look in your pantry—cans of tuna count as meat too!

Step two consists of sitting your pretty little hiney down with the recipe box, coupons, sales ads, scissors, a pen and two pieces of paper—one blank index card labeled "Weekly Menu," and one sheet of paper for your shopping list. Browse the sales ads to find meats on sale that week. If the sales offer includes an abundance of meat, determine how many meals this meat amount will create. A three-pound bag of frozen chicken breasts = two meals for a family of 6 (with small children). With large amounts of meat (5 pounds of ground beef), you can plan two meals that week, then separate the remaining beef into one-pound packages to freeze for later use.

Depending on how many meats you found in your freezer, choose enough meats from the sales ads to total 5-6 meats for the week. Write the meats you need to buy on your grocery list. If you happen to find an *amazing* deal . . . don't be shy buying three or four of the meat packages to freeze for future use. Frozen meat can be kept safely for six months and more.

After you've selected our meats for the week, go to your cookbooks and recipe box. Grab all the recipes you can find which contain the meats you have just compiled on your grocery list. If you are buying pork chops because they are on sale, go to the "pork" category in your recipe box. Skim through the recipes and decide which ones you'd prefer to cook that week. Select five recipes that include meat, and choose one or two meatless recipes for the week as well. Veggie lasagna, homemade veggie pizzas and pasta dishes are all good meatless meal choices. Make at least one super-simple recipe like spaghetti for a day that you may be in ultra-rush mode.

Your menu totals for the week should equal seven meals. If you are on a bi-weekly pay cycle, you'll need to plan fourteen meals to get you through that period. Some recipes will inevitably produce leftovers that we can either eat for lunches, freeze for future use, or transform into a new and exciting recipe! Homemade chili suddenly becomes chilidogs . . . . and it then magically evolves into chili-macaroni! (Darwin would be proud!)

Once you have decided which recipes to cook, write each one on the blank index card you've labeled "Weekly Menu." Leave room for jotting down the side dishes you will serve with each main course, noting whether the recipes are from the recipe box or from a cookbook—otherwise you may forget where you found them. If your recipe comes from a cookbook, document it with something like this: Fettuccine Alfredo, *The Gold Cookbook,* Page 2.

Study each recipe card for ingredients you already have in your home. Then add to your grocery list the items you don't have.

Go back to the store and manufacturer's coupons to see what kinds of "side dishy" food is on sale. Side dishes can be anything from a simple salad, frozen or canned veggie, a rice dish, spaghetti tossed with melted butter and Parmesan, or corn bread served with chili. You will nearly always find that the store brands on sale each week correspond to the manufacturer's coupons offered. I'm assuming the manufacturers notify the stores of their coupon printing and work together on this to stimulate more sales. Decide on seven side dishes and write them on your weekly menu next to your seven main entrees.

After you have chosen your side dishes, search the sales ads for good deals on the fill-in stuff—breakfasts, lunches, snacks, fruit, breads and beverages. You may be able to find manufacturers' and store coupons for many of these items too.

## The Wheels on the Cart Go Squeak, Squeal, Screech . . .

Once you have completed your weekly menu, it's time for the shopping-cart wheels to hit the pavement! Just as the freeway has its rules and regulations—grocery-store shopping benefits from some good common-sense laws too. Follow these simple rules to keep your trip on course:

- *Never go to the store hungry.* Always eat something before you venture out to grocery shop. Do you want a sound mind making shopping decisions for your family, or your grumbling tummy?

- *Stay on the list.* Sticking to the list will save you thousands of dollars over many years. You may want to budget yourself an extra $10.00 each week to purchase deals not advertised in the store ads—such as clearance, overstock, etc.
- *Buy in bulk.* If you are going to buy something used frequently like flour, sugar, oats or rice, consider a ten or twenty pound sack of the stuff! You can store the bag somewhere else in the house and use a smaller container for it in the kitchen. I once bought a bag of yeast from a warehouse store for about $3.50. When I got home, I figured out how much money it would have cost me if had I bought the same amount of yeast in individual packets—it would have cost over $40.00! I'm still using this same bag of yeast four years later.
- *Always buy store-brands whenever possible.* They are almost always the cheapest choice—and most times even less expensive than buying a name-brand item with a coupon. Wal-Mart Super Store has the lowest store-brand prices I've seen yet. I have found the taste and quality of store-brands comparable to that of the well-known labels.
- *Keep your eyes LOW.* The stores tend to put the least expensive items on the very bottom shelves. They are counting on the human tendency to be too lazy to bend down to look at the price or even to pick it up!
- *Bring a calculator.* Even though you have already made out your list, you may just find that even with the coupons you are using—you can still get a better deal on another brand. Unless you're a mathematician, you won't have time to bother with figures—let the calculator do the work.
- *Stock up.* When you find an amazing deal—don't hesitate to buy *ten* of the discounted item. Sometimes grocery stores will feature new items they are market

testing at extremely low prices. Food items may also be sold at clearance prices if they are near expiration or overstocked. If you find pickles for only $.50, and you buy ten jars—you may not have to buy another jar for a whole year! This ends up saving you lots of do-re-mi.

## Mary, Mary Quite Contrary

Vegetable gardening is both a fulfilling and economical way to put nutritious food on your table. By growing your own produce, you can save many trips to the store and bucket loads of bucks. Being wise with seed purchases can limit spending to only pennies per vegetable produced by your garden.

Vegetable gardening does not have to be as time-consuming as one might think. The initial preparation and planting of your garden area is the largest time investment made; after that, you simply need to maintain your area by weeding, watering and fertilizing.

There are even strategies in building your garden which can allow you to grow a weed-free garden. You can create your garden using landscaping cloth which is placed on the ground around the plants. You simply cut X's in the cloth where you wish to plant the seeds, and the seedlings will peek their little heads up through the holes as they mature. The fabric can then be covered with mulch, shredded newspaper or a composting material. The result: no weeds and one delighted mommy!

Growing plants by seed indoors is very simple to do, and ends up saving you cash. I purchase my seed packets for ten cents each. Each seed packet has the potential to create about ten plants. Previously-grown tomato plants usually sell for around $2.00 per plant, and each plant may produce anywhere between 5-8 tomatoes for the season. You can buy the previously-grown plant, which will average about twenty-five cents per fruit grown. By growing your own from seed, you'll spend less than a penny for each tomato harvested. Obviously, the indoor seed method is the most cost-effective, but both ways are certainly less expensive than grocery-store prices.

Many of the items grown in your garden can be frozen and used all year long. Tomatoes can be boiled and chopped or pureed to make spaghetti sauce, tomato paste or diced tomatoes. Canning is no longer necessary with the convenience of gallon or quart-sized plastic freezer bags. Vegetables like cucumbers, peppers, onions and carrots can be chopped up and frozen in plastic bags too. Winter squash can be stored in your pantry or basement for many months after harvest, blessing your family with fresh and delicious squash year-round.

Not only is vegetable gardening inexpensive, but I believe you will find it a wonderful way to spend your time. There is nothing more fulfilling than running out to your very own garden and accumulating everything you need to create a delicious salad for dinner.

Vegetable gardening can also be a fun family activity. The kids can help in the garden by digging, planting seeds, watering, and also weeding. So many valuable life-lessons can be learned by children in the gardening process—patience, work ethic, responsibility, etc. Your family will love taking part in the best part of all—harvesting! So, make it a family affair—and get to tillin' that ground up, Mary!

## Scratch Yourself Silly

With a little knowledge and effort, we can create food items from scratch that most of us usually buy at the grocery store. This can be a very economical habit, saving the added expense on our grocery bills. Here are a few of the food items we can very easily create ourselves:

Taco Seasoning:          Combine 6 tsp chili powder, 4 1/2 tsp cumin, 2 1/2 tsp garlic powder, salt and pepper. Combine all and store in small container. (Buy spices in bulk containers at warehouse stores for the most savings.)

Tartar Sauce:    Combine mayonnaise and relish.

Broth:    Buy beef and/or chicken base, sold in jars at the grocery store, and dissolve in water. Eliminates the need to buy canned broth.

Gravy:    Use meat grease or oil, and while cooking over medium heat, add enough flour to mix into a doughy ball. Then add cold water, mixing with whisk until smooth. Continue adding water while whisking until gravy is desired consistency. Flavor with salt, pepper and beef or chicken base. Dissolved boullion will also work.

Alfredo Sauce:    1/4 cup butter, 1 cup cream, 2/3 cup parmesan cheese (shredded), salt and pepper. Melt butter and add cream and cheese. Stir and simmer for 5 minutes. Turn heat off and stir. Salt and pepper to taste.

Cocktail Sauce:    Combine ketchup and horseradish.

Teriyaki Sauce :    Combine soy sauce, ginger, garlic powder, and sugar. This makes a great sauce for stir fry. Add diluted corn starch to mixture—it will thicken as it cooks.

Psuedo Rice-A-Roni: Heat 4 tblsps of oil in a large frying pan over medium heat. Break a handful of spaghetti or angel hair pasta into small two inch pieces. Combine pasta and 2 cups rice in pan. Brown, stirring occassionally. Add 4 cups water, 1 tblsp beef or chicken base (whichever you prefer), garlic, salt and pepper to taste. If you wish to make Spanish rice, add the water, a can of diced tomatoes, and the above recipe for taco seasoning instead.

Sweet & Sour Sauce: In a saucepan, combine 1/2 cup water, 1 cup ketchup, 1/4 cup sugar, 1 tblsp vinegar. In a separate container, combine 1 tsp corn starch with 1 tblsp water. Combine corn starch mix with ingredients in sauce pan. Bring all ingredients to a boil. Let cool and serve with eggrolls, or cream cheese puffs.

Stuffing: 6 cups cubed bread from leftover heels, 1 tblsp parsley, 3 tblsp chicken base, 1/4 cup dried minced onion, 1 tsp thyme, 1 tsp pepper, 1/2 tsp sage, 1/2 tsp salt. Bake bread cubes @ 350° for 8-10 minutes. Cool and toss with dry ingredients. Store in a closed container. When ready to cook, combine 2 cups stuffing with 1/4 cup water and 2 tblsp butter. Either bake in oven with bird, microwave partially covered for 5-7 minutes, or cook on stovetop for 15-20 minutes or until all water is absorbed.

# Quibble While You Work

*"A bargain is anything a customer thinks a*
*store is losing money on."*
—*Kin Hubbard*

If we take a bit of time, we can find ways to save money on even the most basic items in our homes. Cleaning, household and beauty products can either be created from scratch, purchased at a bargain price, or made to last longer by using simple techniques.

If you make simple habit changes to many areas of your household at once, the total savings can really blow you away. Saving $5.00 a month on laundry soap doesn't seem like a lot of money, but over the course of a year, that $5.00 multiplies.

Many of the household products we use can be made in our kitchens for pennies on the dollar. Below are a list of some useful household recipes:

Laundry Soap:   Ingredients: 1 bar Ivory soap, 1 cup Arm & Hammer washing soda (found in grocery stores by the laundry items). Set aside an old kettle to use solely as your laundry pot. Grate the Ivory soap bar into the kettle with a cheese grater or paring knife, add enough water to cover the grated soap. Bring to a boil, stirring constantly. Reduce heat and continue to stir until soap is dissolved. In the bathtub or sink, fill the five-gallon pail with hot water almost to the top, leaving about three inches unfilled. Add the soap mixture to the bucket, stirring as you add. Add 1 cup washing soda to the bucket, and mix. Pour mixture into one gallon containers (milk or juice jugs work well), leaving room at the top for the soap to expand. Option: You may also add essential oils such as lavender oil to mixture for a stronger scent. The mixture will become gelatinous the next day after cooling completely.

Faux Windex:    Using your old Windex or other bottle, fill halfway with water, a quarter full with ammonia, and a quarter full with vinegar. Put the cap on and mix well.

Baby Wipes:    Gather two empty cylindrical baby wipe holders, the kind with a lid on the top and an X where the wipes come out. Buy a more expensive brand of paper towel such as Bounty, and cut one roll in half using a serrated knife. Remove the cardboard paper tube from the interior of the roll. Place the half-rolls in the bottoms of the containers. Fill the containers with the following solution: 4 cups water, 1 tblsp shampoo, 1 tblsp hair conditioner, and one tblsp baby oil. Close the container and shake back and forth until paper towels are saturated. (Add more water if needed.) Pull a sheet of paper towel from the center of the roll and push it up through the X in the top of the container. You can buy the expensive paper towels with a coupon to save extra money!

Toilet/Tub Cleanser: Use a box of baking soda in place of Comet or other cleaners. You can use it to effectively clean tubs, toilets and sinks. Also safer for children—with no chemicals to worry about.

The lifespan of the products we use in our homes can be stretched by using some thrifty conservation techniques:

- *Cut your dryer sheets into fours.* For each load, use one fourth of a sheet. You will not notice a difference in your laundry. For sheets and blankets . . . I may throw in two-fourths.
- *Use less than the package calls for.* If the package tells you to use one cup of solution . . . try using half of a cup instead. I use this technique with laundry and dishwasher soap; it works great and extends the life of the product.
- *Refill hand-soap containers with old shampoo.* The myth of "anti-bacterial" soap products has been revealed by consumer-product testing companies. *Every* soap has anti-bacterial properties, including shampoo. If you have old bottles of unused shampoo lying around the house, use them as hand soap. It works great.
- *Dig out that lipstick.* Use a lip brush to gain access to the remainder of lipstick in the tube after the point has worn down. There is enough lipstick in that hole to last a good month, or maybe two!
- *Use newspaper to wipe windows and mirrors.* You have old newspapers in the recycling bin . . . so why not put them

to work? Newspapers actually work better than anything else for wiping mirrors and windows, and you don't need to spend any extra money for paper towels.

- *Fill your washers and dryers to maximum capacity.* By putting wimpy little loads in your washers and dryers, you end up wasting time, excess electricity, water, laundry soap and dryer sheets. Fill those babies up! Why would you want to do five loads of laundry when you can condense them into three?

- *Don't buy paper plates or cups unless you're entertaining.* Paper products can be a constant drain on our household budgets. They may be convenient, but not really necessary. If overwhelming dish loads are a problem, train your husband and children to keep one drinking glass for the whole day. Mark their names on wide rubber bands and each day wrap them around their cups. This system can save room in your dishwasher and eliminate the need for paper products.

- *Use toilet paper to wipe your nose.* Why waste your money on tissue paper when T.P. works just as well? In the same way, buy either paper napkins or paper towels, you can use *one* to serve both purposes. Our family has actually survived for ten years having only bought tissue two or three times. Imagine that!

- *Darn your socks, darn it.* Why throw away perfectly decent socks when they have one teensy-weensy little microscopic hole in them? Take three minutes and get out your needle and thread . . . the sock will probably live for another six months. You then have my permission to kill him by cutting him up into pieces and putting him to work as a useful garage rag!

- *Wear your clothes three times.* If your clothing is not visibly soiled or detectably smelly, you can wear it three times before having to put it in the wash. This saves time, money and the extra wear and tear on your clothes.

# "Oh, Martha . . . your house is *so* purty!"

*"The best way to keep children home is to make the
home atmosphere pleasant—and let the air out of the tires."*
—*Dorothy Parker*

Creating a stylish haven that your husband can't wait to come home to does not have to empty your pocketbook. There are many low-priced avenues to finding furnishings and accessories for your home.

Paint is one of the cheapest ways to add a new look and feel to our homes. A beautiful warm tone on the walls can bring a sense of sophistication to the home. You can find "oops" paints at any home improvement store for about $2.00 per gallon. If you check out the discount shelves frequently, you are bound to finally find the color for which you've been looking. One gallon of paint can cover an average bedroom.

The price of prepared window treatments can be overwhelming—especially to the stay-at-home mom on the P. B. & J. budget. Creating your own window treatments is an easy way to get more bang for your buck. If you don't know how to sew, there are many types of treatments that require no sewing, such as cornices, and even fabric shades that can be created using hot glue or fusible webbing (an iron-on adhesive). If you have a friend or family member with sewing skills, by bartering tasks you can get custom treatments very inexpensively. Many fabric stores offer percentage-off coupons or seasonal sales at which you can buy your fabric at a reduced rate. Personally, I take advantage of 50% off coupons offered by a local fabric store, and buy patterns once a year when they offer them at an annual sale for $1.00 a piece!

When looking for furniture at garage sales or thrift stores, only focus on the *form* or *style* of the object you want. Disregard the item color and the fabric style, it can always be repainted or easily recovered with another fabric. I have actually found some of my most favorite furniture pieces in the garbage or on the side of the road. With a little paint and some new fabric, some of them have been the most complimented items I own. Something once hideous-looking can become a beautiful keepsake by simply observing the potential of the frame or design of the piece and bringing it to life. You don't have to be especially creative to do this—all you need is the ability to use a paintbrush and staple gun. It doesn't take much to copy what other creative minds have already done.

If you prefer to buy your furniture new, you can certainly begin a savings envelope in which you can slowly put away the money needed. Layaway is also a great alternative to financing. It is an extraordinary feeling to bring a wonderful furniture piece home—and to actually *own* it!

Browse home-furnishing catalogs like *Pottery Barn*, or visit upscale home-decor stores to gather creative ideas for your home. It is entirely possible to copy the expensive trends without copying the price. Discover what kind of decor you love and study the style. Ask yourself exactly what it is that you like about the look. Is it the smooth lines, the rich textures, the romantic feeling? You can easily duplicate the same traits in your own home with a little resourcefulness.

In whichever style you prefer to decorate, you are sure to find the things you like at garage sales, thrift stores or at trendy discount stores like Target. Accessories are some of the least expensive things we can buy for our home, but they have a huge impact on the final feel of any space. Picture frames, flower arrangements, and other accessories can also be handmade or better yet, found on clearance for next to nothing! Don't you love it when that happens?

Accessorizing using some of the special items we already own like baptismal gowns and childhood memorabilia can be a great way to bring meaning to your home's decor. Decorating is an adventure in itself—don't forget to enjoy the journey, buying and creating things you truly *love* to fill your precious home.

## Taming the Mane

*"For three days after death, hair and*
*fingernails continue to grow but phone calls taper off. "*
—*Johnny Carson*

There are three things you can count on in life—death, taxes, and the need for a barber. Hair care can be a very costly expense, especially when you have lots of heads in the family needing to be groomed. Here are some tips I've found useful in our family's own *hairy* battle:

- *Limit trips to the salon.* If you have one length hair and no bangs (like me), you really only need your hair professionally trimmed once or twice a year. I go in for my annual haircut right around Christmas time— I've even made one gift certificate to the salon last for two years straight. Although I must admit—I've recently become a "bathroom cutter."
- *Don't dye or highlight your hair.* Whoever said that the natural you isn't good enough? The more you mess around with the natural you—the more it's gonna cost! When you keep your natural hair color in tact, there's no need to fret . . . your roots are *always* showing . . . and it's *okay!* If you are dyeing to cover gray, you can do it yourself or have a friend help you by using over-the-counter hair-coloring products. Just make sure you dye your hair a color close to your natural shade, which will eliminate the need for constant root touch-ups.
- *Cut your children's hair yourself.* In our family, we have four boys—and we all gather 'round the VCR three

or four times a year for their snazzy haircuts. I learned to cut my children's hair by carefully observing a stylist during my son's haircuts, checking out a library book on how to cut hair, and by asking my best friend Cally who is a stylist to show me some techniques. It's easier than you may think.

- *Use the Flowbee on your hubby!* I know many stay-at-home moms who use the "Flowbee" hair cutting system—it actually works great! It's an easy way for those who are especially nervous about their haircutting abilities. It requires little or no skill, cleans up the mess for you, and you can use it on the kids too. Check eBay for good deals on the Flowbee!

- *Settle for less.* Don't be tricked into thinking that the expensive, brand-name hair-care products contain some secret outer-space serum only attainable by a particular company! Many times the generic brands work just as well and sometimes they work even better! You can find less expensive brands of shampoo, conditioner, mousse and gel right on your grocery-store shelves.

# Shopping for the Fig Leaf

*"Fashion is a form of ugliness so intolerable that
we have to alter it every six months."*
—*Oscar Wilde*

If we aren't aiming to be arrested for indecent exposure—clothing is an expense we must tackle as well. As with all other products, brand-name clothing tends to be overrated and overpriced. When you buy an expensive designer outfit—you are paying extra for the fame of the name, and not necessarily for the quality.

Used clothing functions just as well as new clothing. You can find stylish and used brand-named clothing for a fraction of what you would pay in retail stores. A $50.00 shirt may sell for $.50 at a garage sale . . . and still be like new!

The best places to find used clothing are: garage sales, thrift and consignment stores, overstock or damaged discount stores, retail-store clearance racks and even in dumpsters! (Okay . . . I know I'm pushing it!) My personal rule of thumb is not to ever pay more than $5.00 for new clothing and shoes (on clearance racks), and at garage sales, to keep each individual clothing piece to under $1.00 if possible.

When shopping for clothing, whether new or used at a garage sale, be sure to compose a list of the things you truly need. Without a list, we can be easily distracted from our goals and return home with tons of stuff we already have or don't really need.

If you know a tasteful woman who is about your size, or if you know a family who has children of the same sex that are older than yours—don't hesitate to let them know that you would appreciate their hand-me-downs. Once people know that you are a willing outlet for their things, they will even have people they know give stuff to you. What you can't use, you can pass along to others. A river that is flowing full of blessings remains fresh—but a pond which keeps its resources to itself stagnates and has no room for more.

## Stirring the Nerd in You

*"A computer once beat me at chess,*
*but it was no match for me at kick boxing."*
—*Emo Philips*

I know we've all been forced to believe that we absolutely *must* have the latest in computer and electronic equipment in order to survive. You've heard the saying, "Computers become outdated the minute they leave the store with you." If your livelihood is earned in the computer industry—this saying may be true for you. But if you are the average computer user who just wishes to do a little online surfing, buying, and maybe sending an email or two—it is not necessary for us to own the latest in computer technology.

If you are in the market for a computer, buying old computers on eBay or from a computer recycler is definitely the best way for the average computer user to go. You can buy a two or three-year-old computer with wonderful Internet capabilities, that will suit the average family very well. You may also land a fantastic computer find at a garage sale if you're lucky.

Many companies upgrade their computers quite frequently, and then proceed to give their old computers away. Don't hesitate to ask your circle of acquaintances to notify you if their company upgrades their system. Two of our computers have come to us this way for free.

The marketing departments of major computer manufacturers purposefully attempt to instill feelings of insecurity about the computer you already own. They've realized that discontentment planted in the hearts of the people equals overflowing dollars in their pockets. Don't allow the mantra of the marketers to seep into your psyche— use your own judgment based on what the technological needs of your own family truly are.

## Let's Go Surfin' Now . . .

*"WARNING: Keyboard Not Attached.*
*Press F10 to Continue."*
*—Anonymous*

Merging onto the ol' super information highway to shop can help you keep bundles of dough in your pockets. I have found the Internet to be an amazing resource for our family. We have used the Web to buy everything from home school books to clown shoes. Some of the benefits of online shopping are:

- Never needing to leave your home to buy stuff (no gas used, no time wasted, no road safety issues).
- Never paying sales tax if the items are purchased from another state.
- Convenient shopping hours . . . the stores never close!
- The opportunity to buy used items from a broader market. You'd have to visit a thousand garage sales to score what you can find during one visit to eBay.

There are a few Internet Service Providers (ISP) that offer limited dial-up Internet connections absolutely free. Using their server, most of these free ISP's will allow you to be connected to the Web for about ten hours per month at no charge, and they include a free email account as part of the package. If you exceed your free ten-hour limit, the ISP will usually charge for any time over the free hour limit. Documenting time spent on the Net will help keep your connection free. Here are some of the free ISP's available:

- www.access-4-free.com
- www.juno.com
- www.netzero.com

Auction sites like eBay are extremely helpful for families on a budget. Not only can you purchase super-cheap used items on eBay, you can use the site to sell your own stuff. With little more than a digital camera and some gumption, you can earn extra money for your family. Sales on eBay require a very small time investment, and you can begin by selling all the extra stuff you have around the house.

Shopping for books online has saved our family oodles of bucks. Amazon.com offers the most amazing deals on used books that I have personally seen. On the Amazon site, independent booksellers offer used versions of almost all books featured. After going to their Website, simply type in the title of the book you're looking for, and when the book information pops up on the screen, look for the text, "Buy Used." I have purchased $15.00 books for $1.50, and know of others who found the sought titles listed at forty cents! You can expect to pay anywhere from $3.00-$5.00 for shipping, but you still get a better deal than from anyplace else.

Whatever you are looking for, it can most likely be found cheaper on the Net. The online retailers do not need to pay for clerks and storefronts thereby passing the savings onto the consumer. It's as simple as typing the name of what you need into the search engines' search field. A worldwide virtual garage sale . . . right at your fingertips. Surf's up, dude!

## Gathering the ol' Cart-n-Bull

*"If all the cars in the United States were placed end to end,*
*it would probably be Labor Day Weekend."*
—*Doug Larson*

It has been a well-documented fact that when we drive a brand-new vehicle off of the lot, the value of the car has already depreciated by thousands of dollars. If we bought a new vehicle, then one week later tried to sell it—it would not be possible to regain the amount we had paid for it. It is now considered "used." Used vehicles sell for considerably less than new vehicles—not because they work any less well, but simply because they can't be called "new."

Purchasing a used vehicle is one of the keen moves we can make as wise consumers. If we are cautious in our research, we can secure a fantastic roadster for plenty less than we'd spend on a new one. The best bet is to find a used car for which we can pay cash, eliminating the need for financing. If you don't have the cash available, a 401K loan can make good sense in purchasing an older vehicle. Many banks will not finance anything older than five years without classifying it as a *personal* loan, which demands higher interest. Borrowing from yourself through a 401K loan can save you tons in interest, and when you pay the loan off, you've just put money back into your savings account! Rockin' system, dude.

Check out roadsides, newspaper classified ads, and message boards for used vehicle sales. You may even know someone selling an older vehicle who would be willing to make payment arrangements with you—provided your reputation is good!

Researching the purchase of a used vehicle can be an easy process if you look in the right places. Make use of a publication such as *Consumer Reports,* it's available at the library—for free! For a complete guide on purchasing used vehicles, check out this Website: www.samarins.com.

When we own an older vehicle—we need only be financially prepared for it to require repairs. (Refer to the sub-chapter "Expect the Unexpected.") "Adult" cars need a little extra T.L.C. (Transmission-Linkage-Carburator) It is wise to maintain enough money in your emergency fund to cover the cost of a new engine if things happen to go sour.

The second car may be purchased for $500-$2000 *without* a loan and used solely as a means of transportation to and from work for your husband—a "junker." Other than low self-esteem or pride issues, there is no need for the second vehicle to be elaborate. The small non-gas guzzling compact can cost-effectively carry your husband to and from his work destination just as well as any spendy S.U.V.

Recently featured on *Good Morning America,* the Economides family which includes five children, revealed their strategy for a no-debt car purchase: they pay themselves a car payment every month, just as they would if they truly owed one, and stock the psuedo payment into their savings account. When they need a new vehicle, they pay cash for it . . . and *voila!* No need for financing! Check out their helpful website on the Internet: www.homeeconomiser.com.

One of the many benefits of owning your vehicles without a loan is the ability to carry liability insurance as opposed to full-coverage. Although we outright own both of our vehicles, we personally choose to carry full-coverage. You may choose to carry liability only—but the cool part is, that it is *your* choice, and not the decision of the bank. Isn't freedom grand?

# A Place to Park Your Testosterone

*"When Solomon said there was a time and a place for*
*everything he had not encountered the problem of*
*parking his automobile."*
—*Bob Edwards*

Okay, time for a few grunts, groans and belches as we discuss the topic of "manly garage stuff." We just can't leave this chapter without discovering helpful hints to assist our husband's [nag our husband's to their deaths] regarding the useful tools [ridiculous guy-fluff we can't stand] they keep in their masculine havens [the place where they feel most comfortable while scratching themselves]—the garage. There are many tools needed to maintain a home, but there are many low-cost ways to purchase these tools.

The need to cut our lawn can be fulfilled with the purchase of a rebuilt lawnmower. Often you can find free lawn mowers being given away on the side of the road. They may work just fine, requiring little more than a tune-up. People generally wonder what to do with old mowers once they replace them with new ones. If you know of anyone who has empty-nesting parents who are moving to a condo or townhome, ask about their lawn mower to see if they are willing to sell it for a good price. Many tools are reasonably priced at garage sales and thrift stores. Use your bargaining skills to swing a terrific deal on a slightly loved weed-whacker.

Tools make great gift suggestions for your gift lists. If your husband has a birthday coming up, or if someone asks him what he'd like for Christmas—needed garage tools make a nice gift recommendation.

Boats, A.T.V.'s and other man toys can also be purchased used at practical prices. If it is his desire to own one of these rootin' tootin' masculine accessories, you can use the same principles previously mentioned for the purchase of a car or truck. Search newspaper classifieds and message boards for good deals on recreation vehicles. You may have to save your money for a while until you are ready for the big buying day . . . but if it is worth having—it is worth waiting for. (Hey—didn't I hear my *Grandma* say that?)

# Chapter Four

## NOW THAT YOU'RE HOME

*"Parents are often so busy with the physical rearing of children that they miss the glory of parenthood, just as the grandeur of the trees is lost when raking leaves."*
—*Marcelene Cox*

Okay—we're home with our babies—now what the heck do we do with them? What in the world are we gonna do with all these hours in a day?

## Clock Watchers

*"A man with a watch knows what time it is.*
*A man with two watches is never sure."*
—*Segal's Law*

There is a common misconception that comes along with the decision to stay home with your children; once you are home, you will have so much time on your hands! Anyone

96

who is a stay-at-home mom knows this is farther from the truth than Sri Lanka is from Little Rock.

We are intended by God to live a life of order, and order must be a part of our parenting and house management as stay-at-home parents. This is a daunting full-time job, with no time clock to punch at the end of the day. If we don't get some sort of grasp on the events in our days, chaos will inevitably reign, and you will feel as if you have less time available than you did when you were working full time outside the home.

I am speaking from a perspective of a woman who enjoys order and organization, but am not by nature a person with these traits abounding in my persona. I am the creative type, and tend to use the right side of my brain more than the left. Order and organization are something that God is constantly allowing me to add to my life in growing degrees. As I grow as a Christian, I find my skills in this area increase as well. God has grace for even the most scatterbrained moms . . . I am living proof!

There must also be a degree of flexibility involved in our order to keep us sane and agreeable. We cannot allow extremes of leniency and rigidity in our homes. Finding a happy medium is the only way to achieve a state of order that allows us to remain outside of a mental institution. Children are unpredictable, and we have to have grace for their changing stages and relentless mess just as our Father has grace for ours!

Making certain that you as a mother are getting proper sleep and eating suitably is one of the most important things we can do to ensure a sane life for ourselves and our families. Keep caffeine intake to a minimum; too much can make you irritable and edgy. Make sure that you are not getting too much sleep each night, this can be especially easy to do if you have a late sleeper. I find that I feel worse if I get too much sleep rather than too little.

Don't feel guilty about taking a ten minute power nap if needed, it can keep you from tearing the heads off of your children and husband as the end of the day draws near. When each and every trait of my children is causing me to act as though I were demon possessed, I let them know it's time for a power nap! I wake feeling refreshed and much happier—with just enough energy built up to make it through the evening without fizzling out.

Some schedules will naturally fall into place for you right away, such as mealtimes and bedtimes; other tasks may require a little more planning, but it is well worth the effort. Schedule housework, grocery shopping, or bill paying on designated days of the week to avoid being overwhelmed with duties at all times! If you need something special during the week, ask your husband to swing by the store on his way home from work. It is much easier for him to do it alone than for you to load three million kids into the car. This can save you an hour out of your day. Your husband can probably accomplish it in fifteen minutes!

The best advice I can possibly give is to work *really* hard on disciplining yourself to wake up an hour or more each morning before your kids. This allows you time with the Lord, a chance to put the dishes away, and to get dressed without interruption. I had a very difficult time getting to the point in my life where I could get up before the kids. I am so thankful that God has helped me to do this—it is my favorite time of day. Selfish mommy! By giving time to yourself, you are in actuality giving a better YOU to your children. When acquiring this discipline, your life will run much more smoothly and keeping up on housework will be much easier—there's nothing else to do before the sun comes up! Try it for a few weeks—I don't think you'll ever stop!

Take your job as a stay-at-home mom as seriously as you would any job; it's the most important job and ministry you will ever have. Your home is your office, and God is the owner of the company. Your husband is the CEO, you are the vice-president, and your children are your temporary employees on loan from the Lord for a season.

# HI-HO, HI-HO . . .
## It's Over-Scheduling You Know!

*"There cannot be a crisis next week.*
*My schedule is already full."*
—Henry Kissinger

I found myself a culprit of the "overdo your schedule" dilemma, and have had to make some changes to simplify my life. My calendar sometimes looked as though I was suffering from Alzheimer's disease . . . full to the brim with something scheduled every day of the week. This was an exhausting lifestyle, and I have been successful in paring down the overwhelming calendar scribbles; it really wasn't that hard to do! I learned this valuable virtue, "Saying no is an art form." I cannot say that those who know me are pleased by my new semi-hermit status, but I can tell you that I am much less stressed and can properly enjoy my family life now that I have set these boundaries. My children are reaping the rewards of having a mother who now knows how to say no to others.

It is a basic human need to spend time with those we love—friends and family. It is such a benefit to us all to take a break from our normal daily schedule and indulge in a fun day of fellowship with our dear ones. You may find that in order to see *everyone* each month, you'll have to schedule time with all the people in your life once or twice a week! Pretty soon . . . there's no time left for the family! If you're having trouble seeing everyone and staying on top of life, some boundaries in this area must be drawn.

How about scheduling play-dates or time with more than one friend at the same time? Invite two or three of your friend's with kids out to the park for a picnic. Your kids will get to play, and you and your friend's can jabber up a storm simultaneously!

Designating one day a week or two times a month to visiting

time can help you avoid over-scheduling commitments. On a trip to a rural Amish town with my husband, I discovered that the simple Amish folk have a tradition for fellowship that I found interesting. They go to church on two Sunday's a month, and the other two Sunday's they call "visiting Sunday". I found this idea to be a great one! We could all use a little of the Amish touch in our lives.

Many parents over-schedule their children in activities and commitments; I believe this to be a habit that tears families apart, discouraging cohesiveness. Spending your life behind the wheel of a vehicle while eating hand-held soup products and various other fast meals in the car is not a family-oriented lifestyle by any means. Involve each child in only one activity per season to avoid this mad fiasco. Children can play sports with their neighborhood friends in the backyard to fulfill exercise and sportsmanship needs. Sentencing yourself to a life as a taxi driver has no payoffs. Your kids will be just fine without being involved in *every* imaginable activity. Give them a chance to show how creative they can be in filling their own schedules!

## Satan on Line Two!

*"Television has proved that people will look*
*at anything rather than each other."*
—Ann Landers

I am writing this sub-chapter as a warning to all moms about the dangers involved in the overuse of our wonderful technologies. This includes the computer, television and phone. We humans are very susceptible to technological distractions, and the subtle neglect of our children attributed to these devices is a universal problem that many of us do not even notice.

I recently heard a statistic that I found quite alarming. The study stated that an average American family spent about

49 hours a week watching television and only 35 minutes per week in meaningful conversation with their children. I hope that I am not the only one who is appalled by this finding. Appalled, but not surprised!

Television can be a wonderful means of education for the family and can also provide an occasional escape from reality. Many homes overuse this technology and use the device as a babysitter. Some women are mesmerized by the set, leading them to inactivity and procrastination in family matters.

The television can be a form of neglect of our children if we are watching it more than we are watching them, or if we are half-listening to the things they say as we focus on the tube. If the television is on all day, you'd better rethink your priorities. Most experts say that one hour a day of television for children is ample, and that anything more can lead to many problems, including obesity and being easily distracted.

If you are having problems controlling the television watching in your home, you may want to consider a television fast—a social cleansing time. Remove the television from your home for two weeks, or one month. You may find that you like its absence so much, you never want it back! However, upon bringing the television set back into the home, you will be fully aware of how much you relied on it and how much it was overused.

One idea that I've found helpful in controlling the technology time was to create T.V. coupons for each child. At the beginning of the week, each child is given his or her coupons for seven hours of T.V. or computer time. Each time they decide to watch T.V. or play the computer, they must first ask, then redeem their coupons to Mom or Dad. When they redeem their coupons, hand them an egg timer that is set for the amount of time allowed. This is a fair way of keeping track of the kids viewing and computer games without arguments. It may be helpful to you.

Another technology monitoring technique I've recently stumbled upon is the "Reading/Technology Trade." It works like this: If a child reads for thirty minutes, they can then indulge in thirty minutes of computer/television/video game use. They can read for as many hours as they'd like to build up their time, and simply subtract the minutes as they watch/play their favorite technology. This method is fantastic. The child feels as if they are in control of their own technology schedule, and doesn't blame Mom for their inability to watch/play. My children have even been utilizing their time as we drive to and fro in the van to read and earn technology minutes.

The Internet can be a major addiction to many men and women with it's vast informational capacity. The lure of the information superhighway can drag us away from our children in a very cunning way. If you find yourself hopping on the computer just to check your email "real quick," then end up surfing the Net—being distracted by every twist and turn the Internet leads you in, you need to set a self-control goal. Train yourself to *just* check your email.

Try to limit your Internet surfing to after the kids are in bed before they get up in the morning. The small amount of time we have with our children is so precious, it will not be a happy memory to look back on our wasted time when we had nothing but visions of eBay dancing in our retinas. Wouldn't you rather remember dancing with your children? Me too!

The telephone probably tops the list of overused devices in the lives of mothers today—the most common form of child neglect. We are all social beings and have a need for adult interaction, but our children deserve to be paid attention to, and deserve to have a mother who exercises self-control.

The phone was created to relay useful information in a timely way. It is quite a step-up from the old-fashioned way of sending telegrams or using the pony express. Most messages of importance can effectively be communicated in three minutes or less, yet we find ourselves beyond our initial intent, engrossed in superfluous conversation. We suddenly realize we've just wasted an hour of our day while our children are in the background doing God knows what?! (My two year old likes to pour out the spices when mommy is on the phone!)

The phone is a time thief at work in the daily lives of many humans—not just stay-at-home moms. Please be aware of the time you are on the phone and of your children's reaction when they see you on the phone. If they turn into raging animals the second they see the receiver lifted to your ear—this is a sign that they are accustomed to your overuse of the phone.

Sometimes the urge to talk to those in the outside world is so overwhelming. If you have difficulty in keeping conversations to a minimum (which I do), set a timer when you get on the phone and discipline yourself to get off when you hear it ring. I am the queen of the answering machine! I do this because I believe it is unfair to my children to be neglected constantly by my phone use or to have their bedtime or naptime storybook interrupted by a meaningless chat. If the phone call is important, the person is bound to leave a message, and you can call them back when it is convenient for the family. This does not mean that you love the person making the phone call any less. It's just good time-management, setting our priorities in order.

I occasionally indulge in conversations, but I try to do this during nap times or after kids are in bed. Obviously, there are exceptions when friends or family are going through tough times and need you to minister to them or just to listen. But on most occasions, convey your thoughts in a brief way, and then get back to your family.

# Raising Your Little Adults

*"Children are natural mimics; they act like their parents
in spite of every effort to teach them good manners."*
—*Author Unknown*

Even though the term is generally coined "raising children," in actuality, we are truly "raising adults." If we focus on this goal, it will help us to rear children fully prepared to enter the world upon reaching eighteen or sooner to be successful, responsible, and ready to give of themselves to their community and to God's work.

How tempting it is to overlook behaviors in our children, deeming them as "childish habits" that will pass with age. Each child is born with natural areas of weakness in character and personality. It is our job to help them develop those areas into areas of strength NOW when the consequences of mistakes are still small. Neglecting this priority can result in serious turmoil and pain in your child's adult life.

Some of these areas include, but are not limited to: poor eating habits, irresponsible money handling, laziness, excessive television watching and video game playing, whining, complaining and grumbling, anger, weak self-control, disrespect to others, disobedience to parents which can soon become disobedience to the Lord and many others.

Find Biblically-based books for those areas of struggle. Equip yourself to assist your child in overcoming his or her area of weakness through prayer and knowledge. Your child will thank you for it.

Our children were not placed in our care here on earth solely for the purpose of taking them to the carnival once a year. We are responsible for turning out children capable of handling anything that life has to throw at them. Although being a friend to your child is a lot of fun, it is not our responsibility. Our children will have friends in their lives, but they need their parents to be parents. They need guidance, love and security from us.

Give your children household duties to perform as part of their daily lives without reward. This makes them feel important and needed. They do the work because they are a part of the family unit.

Teaching them *real life* includes showing them that when something becomes dirty, someone has to take responsibility to clean it. You can train them to automatically think that Mother will be the one to clean a dirty item when needed, but you are certainly setting yourself up for a scolding from your future sons and daughters-in-law after they have taken your place as slave.

Small children can do easy chores such as dusting, rinsing dishes in the sink, and folding laundry. Older children can handle bigger jobs like loading and running the dishwasher, sweeping the floor, vacuuming and mopping. Training your children to be helpful around the house has too many benefits to list, but some critical ones include selflessness, consideration, a good work ethic, taking pride in their work, family cohesiveness, and serving others. It also makes for a smiling mommy who is not overburdened by doing the work of the family—when others in the family are responsible for it as well.

# Now to Conclude, Dude

*"From the moment I picked up your book until I*
*laid it down, I was convulsed with laughter.*
*Some day I intend reading it."*
—*Groucho Marx*

We as women have experienced many benefits from the feminist movement—the right to vote, and the right to have access to well-paying jobs and education. I am thankful to those who've battled for the equality of women, but am uncertain whether those tough cookies who rallied for our rights during the suffrage ever imagined that as women gained many freedoms—they would also eventually lose the right to raise their own children at home.

The postwar era placed women in the workforce and introduced to the culture mass production and the installment plan. What initially seemed like an anticipated waterfall of independence soon became enslavement—driving down the pay scales of men and leading to increased pressure for women to earn an income. Women who once enjoyed the new freedoms of being able to *choose* employment were now being compelled into positions they no longer wanted to possess. Thus, the freedom of choice soon evolved into financial dependence.

This trend has continued throughout American society for more than thirty years after World War II. Many husbands still embrace the expectation that their wives are required to work if they are to make ends meet. This mindset has thankfully begun to cease over the last decade—but still many men and women are enslaved by these philosophies of modern living.

As this book concludes, my prayerful hope is that a new and fulfilling chapter in your lives will begin to unfold. The journey before you is one that includes both painful sacrifice and intangible gain—yet I am convinced that being home with your children *can* become a reality for you.

Our responsibility to our children is not to be taken lightly—as it is the most vital liability we will ever encounter. We now have the opportunity to take a stand for the mothers of this nation, and to be a voice for the children who are not heard. Our choice to rear this generation of children at home will pave the way for the daughters of tomorrow to do the same. Don't ever give up the fight for your right to raise your own children.

# Endnotes

## Chapter One

(1) Dr. Kevin Leman, *Bringing Up Kids Without Tearing Them Down*, p. 78.

(2) National Institute of Child Development [NICHD] Study of Early Child Care in the November 1999 issue of *Developmental Psychology*.

(3) Kelly, R.J. (2000).

(4) J. Froom, "Antimicrobials for Acute Otitis Media? A Review from the International Primary Care Network," *British Medical Journal 315* [July 12, 1997] p.98-102.

(5) Diane K. McHale, "Talking about Childcare: What's the Research Really Say?," *Mothering Magazine*, Issue 112, May/June 2002.

(6) National Institute of Child Development (NICHD) Study of Early Child Care in the November 1999 issue of *Developmental Psychology*.

(7) P.J. Louhiala, "Form of Daycare and Respiratory Infections Among Finnish Children," American Journal of Public Health 85, no. 8 (1995) p.1109-1112.

(8) "Day Care Information: Effects on Infants Emotional Development," *Pagewise©*.

(9) Marilyn Elias, "More Kids in Declining Daycare," *USA Today*, November 7, 1991.

(10) Edgerton, Jane E. 1994. *American Psychiatric Glossary, 7th Edition*. Washington, DC: American Psychiatric Press.

(11) Hoffman, M.L., *Stages of Guilt Development*, Looksmart, Ltd.©(2004).

(12) The American Heritage® Dictionary of the English Language, Fourth Edition, Copyright © 2000 by Houghton Mifflin Company. Published by Houghton Mifflin Company.

(13) Handford, Elizabeth Rice, *Me? Obey Him?*, Sword of the Lord Publishers, 1994

Visit **www.raisingyourownchildren.com** to:

- Order additional copies of *RAISING YOUR OWN CHILDREN*
- Read stay-at-home mom testimonies—and submit your own!
- Add your own online book review
- Learn more about the Raising Your Own Children Workshop
- Gain access to useful links and resources—cheap recipes too!
- Contact author, Carey Keavy